The *New* Sampler Quilt

Diana Leone

Leone Publications
Mountain View, California

To all of my friends, family, and customers who have supported me over the past twenty years. I have seen the quilt world, as we know it, begin in the 70s and grow today to such a refined level that it encompasses and encourages quiltmakers of all levels of development to begin and continue on in this wonderful field.

Working on this book over the past two years has helped me appreciate how many quilters there are out there, and how much you want to learn and produce beautiful quilts.

To all of you, especially the beginner, enjoy quilting, learn, and continue making quilts forever. I invite all of you to visit my store, The Quilting Bee, in Mountain View California, when you are in Northern California. Come in, bring your quilts in progress, and share them with all of us.

Graphic Artist and Senior Editor: Maura McAndrew
Pattern Illustrations: Lynn Dalton
Editors: Carol Baxter, Joan Chamberlain, Joan Freitas, Stevii Graves,
        Joan Pederson, Virginia Schnalle
Illustration page 49 courtesy of Cheryl Bradkin, author *Basic Seminole Patchwork*
Photography: Diana Leone Studio
Additional photography: Tom Moulin, Jeff Munroe and Sharon Risedorph

Cover quilt designed by Diana Leone, pieced by Sondra Rudey,
hand quilted by April Murphy.
Cover design: George Mattingly Design, Berkeley
Printing: PENN&INK/Colorcraft, Ltd., Hong Kong

ISBN 0-942786-41-6
Library of Congress Cataloging-in-Publication Data

Leone, Diana.
The New Sampler Quilt by Diana Leone.
Rev. ed. of The Sampler Quilt by Diana Leone, 1977.
Includes bibliographical references and index.
1. Quilting. 2. Quilting —Patterns. I. Leone, Diana. Sampler quilt. II. Title. TT835.L46
1993
746.9'7—dc20
93-1914 CIP

Leone Publications
Mountain View, California 94041 U.S.A

10 9 8 7 6 5 4 3 2

Contents

Pastel Sampler Quilt designed by Diana Leone. Pieced and hand quilted by Doris Olds.

Twenty some years ago I made my first patchwork block. There were few quilting books, even fewer shops, and almost no quilting classes. I decided to make my first block "Corn and Beans." I chose some yellow and green calico fabrics. I cut the templates (not too carefully) out of cardboard (that was probably too thick). The fabric was marked and cut. The little pieces were hand sewn together. I looked at the finished block and decided that the best solution for this misadventure was a burial in the "pet cemetery" in the back garden. Why did I continue? Because I had found a creative medium that was forgiving, flexible, and challenging enough to hold my interest over the next twenty-five years.

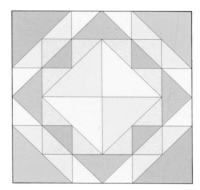

I began my quiltmaking career in 1972 by teaching quiltmaking at San Jose State University. I taught my students to make a Sampler Quilt, which provided a sampler of lessons in design, fabric selection, hand and machine techniques, and finishing. It provided a vehicle to teach a variety of techniques while the students learned sound fundamentals of quiltmaking.

In 1979, as a result of my teaching, I wrote the original *Sampler Quilt*. The first edition of this book was written as a thorough guide to start a beginner on a traditional course in quilting. Since that time, many new tools and techniques have been developed. This new edition has been rewritten to include the latest methods and the newest tools to guide you successfully through the process of making your own Sampler Quilt and/or first quilt.

This book is meant for both beginners and experienced quilters. If you are a beginner, it is my hope that you will learn the best of traditional methods, develop your interest, and continue. Don't become overwhelmed by the largeness of the whole project. Select one pattern. Cut the first block. Piece two pieces together, then the next two, and so on. Soon you'll have made your first block.

The Sampler lessons include thirty-six pieced or appliquéd blocks; each square is 12" finished (12½" unfinished). The patterns are presented in alphabetical order. The number of thimbles indicates the difficulty of the pattern. The list of pattterns in the back of the book is in order of difficulty. You may want to begin by piecing the easiest block, Patience Corner, and make a small quilt, pillow or placemat. Make a wall quilt using two to twelve blocks; use twenty blocks for a twin bed, twenty-five blocks for a double bed, or thirty blocks for a queen- or king-sized bed.

The 90s have brought many fast cutting and piecing techniques. These methods are best used by quilters who have first mastered the traditional skills. After you learn these basics, you will enjoy using and combining all of the latest fast and easy techniques.

If you are an experienced quilter, you will appreciate having all the best tools and techniques described in one reference book. If you are a teacher, you will use this book as a resource to complement your own methods.

Whatever the size of the project you choose, this book will guide you through to its completion. Over the past twenty years, hundreds of quilters have sent in photographs of their first Sampler Quilts. Share your success by sending me a photograph of your quilt; I'd love to see your work. Above all, I hope that you enjoy making your quilt, and that your Sampler Quilt will be the first of many.

Diana Leone

Introduction

What is a quilt? It is a fabric sandwich—fabric on top, a batting filler, and fabric on the back—joined together with quilting stitches and bound around the edges. What is a Sampler Quilt? When the top layer of fabric is a collection of different block designs, appliquéd, pieced, or both, placed together in a planned or random set, it is called a Sampler Quilt. The process of making the Sampler blocks begins and enriches the learning experience. The Sampler becomes the best teaching tool available, allowing the quilter to practice the various piecing and appliqué techniques while enjoying the process of making the thirty-six different blocks.

How to Use this Book

The first section contains a list of supplies to get you started. In all cases, brand names are mentioned when the item has been found to be of excellent quality. Many other brands are available; some are local to your area. Test different products and decide what is best for you. The quilt plans help you determine what size quilt to make. Each size includes yardage estimates. The next section helps you select fabric, make templates and cut the fabric. Use of the rotary cutter and quick cutting methods are illustrated. Instruction is included for piecing by hand or machine, hand appliqué, setting the blocks together, and for marking the top for hand or machine quilting. A section on the quilting process discusses the materials you will need to finish your quilt. The final section includes information on cleaning, hanging and storing your quilt. The thirty-six block designs are full-size and easy to use.

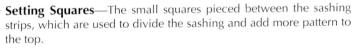

Setting Squares—The small squares pieced between the sashing strips, which are used to divide the sashing and add more pattern to the top.

Patchwork—The process of stitching small pieces together in a planned manner to create a pattern or design. Patchwork is based on grids of a variety of divisions. The patchwork block is the unit formed by the patchwork or appliqué design. The blocks in this book are 12" finished (12½" including the seam allowance). Blocks are placed, or set, together to make a larger pattern—a wallhanging, bed-sized top, etc. There are thousands of designs that may be drafted and made into 12" blocks.

Appliqué—(To lay on) The process of stitching fabric pieces, usually curvilinear, to the surface of another fabric piece. Designs for appliqué are endless.

Sashing/Lattice—The strips of fabric set between blocks used to separate and unify the various blocks.

Border—One or more pieces of fabric sewn around the quilt top's perimeter to form a frame for the top. The border is used to make the top larger without making more blocks. The border may be as simple or complex as you want. The diagram illustrates a variety of border treatments.

"Gwendolyn's Quilt". Colors by Diana Leone. Pieced and quilted by Doris Olds. Note the appliqué of Mother Goose on the Flying Geese block, which shows the technique of patchwork-appliqué, developed by Diana Leone in 1989.

Supplies and Materials

Ironing Board

Use a sturdy, well-padded ironing board. A Pressing Block™ by Tailor Made placed near the sewing machine provides a handy pressing surface.

Iron

A heavy, steam/dry iron is essential for effective pressing. The Rowenta™ iron is one of the best on the market today. The Rowenta travel iron is lightweight, steams, is portable and is great next to the sewing machine for quick pressing.

Rulers

Plastic gridded rulers (2" x 18" and 1" x 6") are used for measuring fabric and templates, and as general guides for marking. Use these rulers to mark any straight sewing or quilting lines. A 2" x 18" C-Thru® ruler is excellent for general marking. Note that the C-Thru® ruler is too soft to use with a rotary cutter.

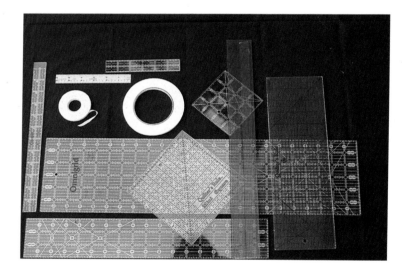

Masking/Drafting Tape

A strip of tape is placed on the surface of the quilt to act as a guide for straight line quilt stitches. The most common tape is ¼" wide; ½" or 1" wide tape may also be used. A ¼" flexible tape is available for curved lines.

Cutting Guide

Many different rigid plastic cutting guides or rulers, in a variety of widths and lengths, are available for use with the rotary cutter. I use Omnigrid® or Quilter's Rule™ cutting guides, 3" x 18" or 6" x 24" with imprinted, easy-to-see horizontal, vertical and angle lines made especially for quilters.

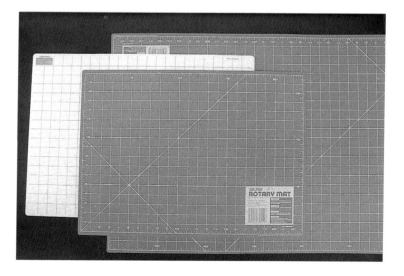

Cutting Mat

Self-healing vinyl cutting mats are used with rotary cutters. These mats come in a variety of sizes with horizontal, vertical and angle lines printed on the surface. A small 6" x 18" mat is a good size for small projects or for taking to classes. Use the 18" x 24" or 24" x 36" mat for the majority of your cutting. A 36" x 72" mat covering an entire work surface is ideal. The Charvoz™ and Olfa™ cutting mats are the longest lasting brands.

Rotary Cutter

The rotary cutter is a sharp, round cutting wheel attached to a handle, and is available in two sizes: large (1¾" diameter) and small (1" diameter). These tools are used with a cutting mat and cutting guide to cut fabric accurately and efficiently. The large rotary cutter is used for cutting multiple layers of fabric. The small rotary cutter is used for one or two layers and curves. I recommend the Olfa™cutter in the large size.

Fabric Markers and Pencils

You will need sharp pencils for marking the pieces and the cutting and quilting lines. Use these pencils on both the right and wrong side of the fabric. The following pencils are suitable for marking on fabric:

- Berol Verithin™ pencils or other washable semi-hard wax-based pencils for marking the right or wrong side of the fabric. The silver and white pencils are the most versatile because they show on both light and dark, prints and solid fabrics.

- Berol Prismacolors® are soft colored pencils that will mark the wrong side of fabrics.

Verithin™ and Prismacolor® pencils are available in over twenty colors and wash out as well as possible.

- Use a mechanical pencil with 3H lead or the SenseMatic® automatic pencil for marking quilting or sewing lines. These pencils stay sharp and allow you to mark close to the edge of the ruler. Lead pencil marks are the most difficult to remove from cotton fabrics—use lightly and with caution.

- General™ Pencil's white charcoal pencil, as well as any brand of chalk markers or even a sliver of soap are suitable markers for quilting and sewing lines.

Test all pencil marks to make sure they can be washed out. Mark lines on the fabrics and wash.

Pencil Sharpener

Keep a small pencil sharpener in your sewing box. A battery-operated or electric sharpener is a great addition to any sewing room.

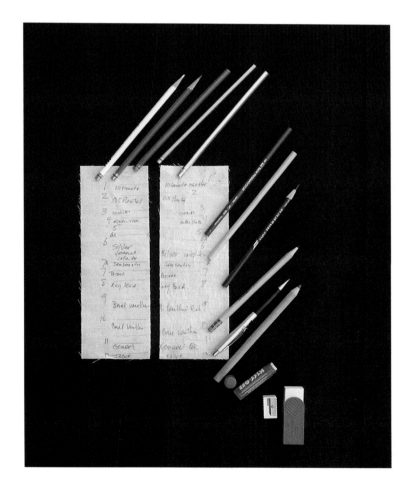

Marking Board

A marking board is a thin ¼" sheet of wood with a piece of fine sandpaper glued to it. The fabric is placed on the sandpaper to keep it from slipping while marking the lines on the fabric pieces. Make a marking board by gluing two 8½" x 11" sheets of fine emery sandpaper onto one side of a 22" x 15" sheet of thin plywood or masonite.

Template Materials

Plastic sheets, 8½" x 11" or 11" x 18", plain or printed with a grid, are used for template material. The pattern piece is traced onto the plastic and then carefully cut with a sharp pair of scissors. Six 8½" x 11" sheets will be enough for all of the patterns in this book.

Plastic Template Markers

Use Sharpie Fine Line® or other permanent felt-tip pens to draw lines on most plastic when making templates.

Envelopes

Use separate envelopes to store each pattern's templates. Write the pattern name, the dimensions of the template (for example: 4" square, 3" triangle base), and page number on the front of the envelope for quick reference.

Labels

Place self-adhesive labels onto each plastic template. Write the pattern name, page number, and how many pieces of each template to cut for the block on each label.

Hole Punch

A ¹⁄₁₆" or ⅛" size metal hole punch is used to make holes where matching dots are marked on the plastic template. A very large (size 16) yarn darner needle can also be used to make holes in the template.

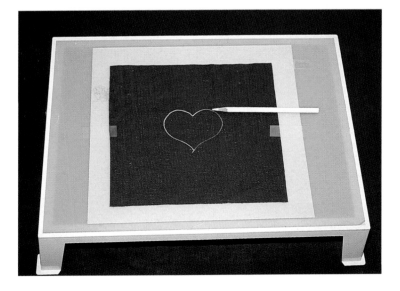

Light Box

A light box is used to provide light behind the quilt top so that the quilting lines can be traced onto the quilt top. Purchase a commercial light box which has a fluorescent light within a box, or make a simple version. One suggestion is to remove one leaf of an adjustable dining table. Place a lamp under the table, and a sheet of glass or rigid, clear Plexiglas™ over the opening. The light box pictured at left is by Me Sew, Inc.

Pin Cushion

The strawberry on top of the pin cushion is filled with sand or hair and can be used to keep the pins and needles sharp. A bar of soap makes a good needle holder and also keeps pins and needles sharp.

Beeswax

A cake of beeswax is used to coat thread for hand quilting. Beeswax prevents the thread from twisting and knotting, and enables the thread to glide through fabric. Any dirt from your hands stays on the surface of the thread and will wash away easily.

Bag Balm

A soothing antiseptic which, when rubbed onto the fingertips, will heal the prick marks made from the needle during the hand quilting process.

Seam Ripper

A seam ripper is a small, sharp, pointed tool used to remove seams. Use the seam ripper to help ease bulky seams between the machine foot and the feed dog, and to remove unwanted seams.

Pins

Short, fine pins with a small round head are used to pin the thin pieces of the cotton fabric together. The Tru Point™ brand by Copper Industries or any thin, fine pin will not distort the fabric pieces or the seam line, and the small head is easy to feel and hold. Long pins with large heads, sometimes called Quilt Pins are best used to pin the thick layers of the quilt together when a thicker (1") batt is used. They are too large and too thick to use to pin small pieces together.

Needle Threader

A needle threader has a small rigid handle with a fine loop of wire at one end. Use the needle threader to thread the small eye of the appliqué and quilting needles. Use a quality threader, as the inexpensive ones break easily. The Clover™, Elna and White™ brands are fine and strong.

Needle Grabber

A needle grabber is a small rubber disk or a small balloon used to pull a needle filled with quilting stitches through the quilt.

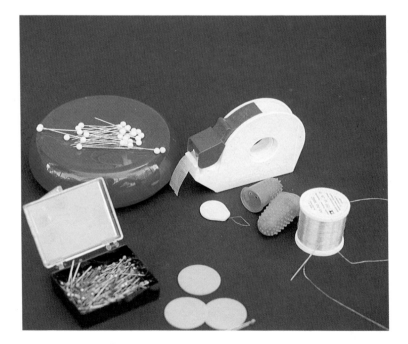

Needles

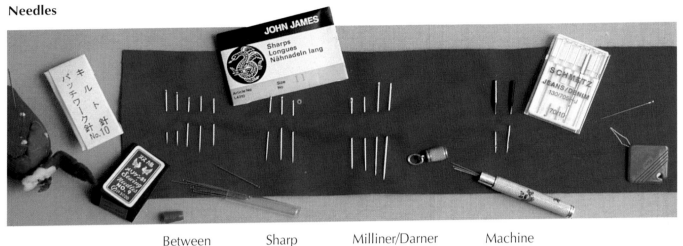

| Between | Sharp | Milliner/Darner | Machine |

"Betweens" are short, sturdy (1"-1¼") quilting needles, sizes 7 through 12, used for hand quilting. The higher the number, the shorter the needle; the shorter the needle, the smaller the stitch. Use the shortest one you can handle. Start with a size 9. Soon after try a 10, and then when you are ready, try a 12.

"Sharps" are long (1¼"-1½"), thin needles used for hand piecing and hand appliqué. Sizes 9 and 10 are suitable lengths for most hand work.

"Milliners" or *"Darners"* are very long (2"-2½"), thin needles in sizes 3 through 9, used for basting.

Most *Sewing machine needles* are made by Schmetz™, and packaged under various names. Use a size 10 or 12 "Jeans" needle for sewing on woven cottons. "Universal" needles have a slightly rounded tip and do not pierce woven cotton as well as the "Jeans" needles. Use a 130N "Top Stitch Needle" for machine quilting. Change the needle about every eight hours of sewing time.

Thread

Use 100% cotton thread or cotton-covered polyester thread for hand or machine piecing, appliqué and hand quilting. The 100% polyester thread is too strong and will break down the fibers of 100% cotton fabric, possibly creating holes in the fabric. "Quilting thread" can be any fine quality thread, as described below. "Basting thread," used for basting the layers of quilt together, can be any white or light-colored thread.

Coats and Clark Dual Duty™ thread is cotton-wrapped polyester, fine and strong, and used for hand or machine work.

Mettler produces a 100% cotton silicon-coated thread available in many colors. This thread is very strong, and is used for piecing, appliqué, and quilting by hand or machine.

Coats and Clark "Quilting Thread" is coated with silicon and is too thick to thread through size 12 quilting needles. This thread is very strong, and is used for hand quilting with longer needles. It should not be used in the machine.

Metallic threads are popular today. Use a short length for hand quilting—10" for example, as this thread may ravel. Sulky makes a metallic thread that can be used for hand or machine quilting. Use Sewer's Aid to lubricate the thread for both hand and machine sewing.

Clear or gray nylon monofilament thread by YLI™ is used as either a top or bottom thread for machine quilting, machine appliqué, for use with decorative threads, and for binding.

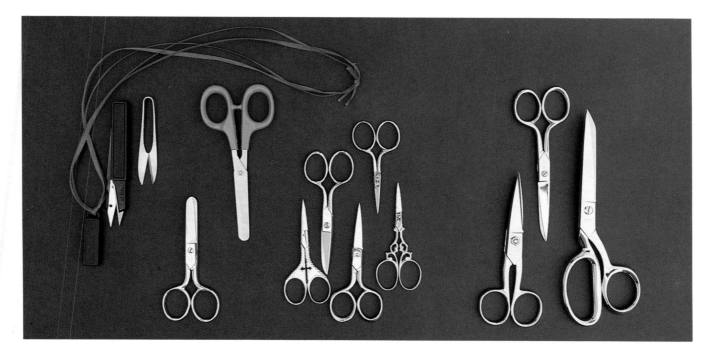

Scissors

A variety of scissors is needed for the quiltmaking process. At a minimum, you'll need sharp dressmaker scissors for cutting fabric, and a pair of sharp scissors for cutting paper, plastic and batting. Use a pair of small scissors for clipping threads. I especially recommend:

- Dressmaker scissors, Gingher® size G7 for general fabric cutting
- Embroidery scissors, Gingher® G5 or G4KE for fine work and at the machine
- Pocket scissors, Gingher® G4B short and blunt, to clip threads
- Thread clippers, used to snip threads

Designate one pair of good quality sharp scissors for cutting paper, plastic and batting. Do not use your fabric scissors for these tasks. Keep all scissors sharp. Your scissors will last a lifetime. Purchase the best you can find.

Thimble

You must wear a thimble for hand quilting. Although it will feel awkward at first, you will get used to it. Try the thimble on. It should feel comfortable on the longest finger of your writing hand. There is a variety of thimbles to try—find the one that feels the best to you.

- A metal thimble with good indents on the sides and bottom is the best to use for hand piecing and quilting. A well-chosen silver thimble has the finest indents and will last a long time.
- A Nimble Thimble™, Knit Kits™, or any soft leather thimble, used as a substitute for a metal thimble, is especially good for beginners who have never worn a thimble. The Nimble Thimble™ also allows for a long fingernail.
- Use two thimbles, one on each hand, as illustrated on page 78.

TIP
Purchase metal thimbles in two sizes, a smaller one for winter and a larger one for summer.

Specialized Sewing Machine Attachments

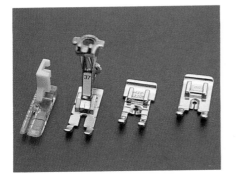

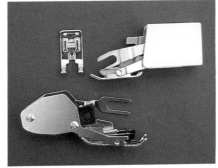

1/4" Quilting Feet

A specialty foot that measures the ¼" seam allowance, this attachment fits most machines, and is available in clear plastic.

Bernina and Viking each manufacture a ¼"-wide quilting foot.

Walking Foot / Dual Feed Foot

A specialty foot that feeds the top and bottom layers through at the same time. This foot is excellent for matching plaids and for applying binding. It is also used for straight line and other machine quilting.

Single Needle Throat Plate and Single Needle Foot

A single needle throat plate and a single needle foot help the machine form a perfect stitch and a smooth seam.

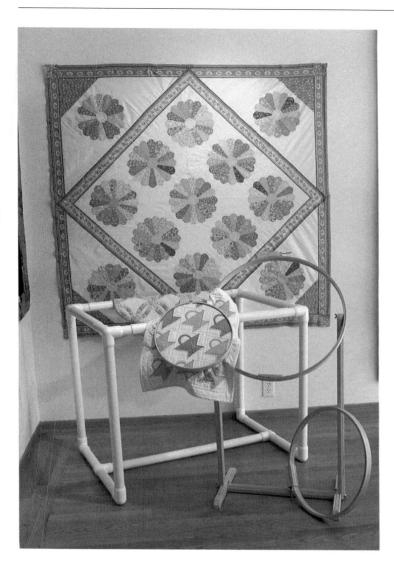

Quilting Frame

The quilting frame holds the quilt taut and off the lap while you are in the process of hand quilting. Quilt frames can be very simple or very elaborate. The Q-Snap™ frame is a set of PVC pipes used to hold the basted quilt. This frame is 27" x 45". It will hold an area of a small to a very large quilt. Smaller sized Q-Snaps™ are used for portability.

There are many excellent wooden floor frames. See Buyer's Source.

Quilting Hoop

Use a 14" or larger round, sturdy quilting hoop. The hoop may or may not have a floor stand. The hoop holds taut the section of the quilt that you are quilting. A hoop can be used for any size quilt. Select a hoop that is comfortable for you to handle easily, and provides the largest area to quilt.

Use the smaller Q-Snap™ hoop, or any wooden Marie™ hoop; they are made of hardwood and are strong enough to hold the quilt taut.

Batting

Batting is the filler that gives loft and warmth to the quilt. Batting is manufactured into sheets for crib, twin, full, queen, and king sizes, as well as by the yard. A 100% polyester low-loft (3.5 oz.), fairly thin batt (approximately ½" thick) is most commonly used for a hand-quilted quilt.

This unseen element is an incredibly important part of the quilt. Purchase bonded or resinated batting manufactured specifically for the fine quilt that you are making. The bonded or resinated batt contains a resin that holds the batting fibers together. The resin should be throughout the batt, not just on the outer surface. Non-resinated batt may "beard." Bearding is the migration of the small polyester batting fibers through the weave of the fabric used on the top and back of the quilt.

There are many brands and types of batt. Hobbs Poly-down® and Fairfield Low-Loft™ are premium battings made for a quilt which will be hand quilted. Hobbs makes a dark batt that is especially suitable inside a quilt made of dark fabrics. Their new wool batt is superb.

Use a thin (¼"), 100% cotton or a cotton-polyester blend made especially for quilts that will be machine quilted. Read the manufacturer's directions for care and quilting instructions.

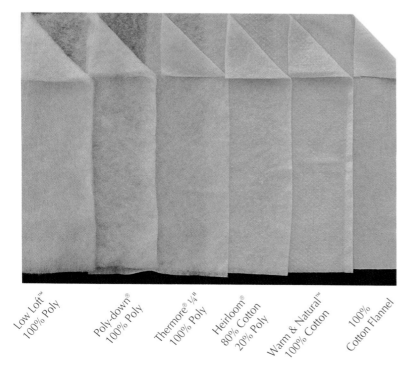

Low Loft™ 100% Poly   Poly-down® 100% Poly   Thermore® ¼" 100% Poly   Heirloom® 80% Cotton 20% Poly   Warm & Natural™ 100% Cotton   100% Cotton Flannel

Estimating Yardage

Yardage

⅛ yd = 4½" (10.8cm)
¼ yd = 9" (21.6cm)
⅜ yd = 13½" (32.4cm)
½ yd = 18" (43cm)
⅝ yd = 22½" (54cm)
¾ yd = 27" (64.8cm)
⅞ yd = 31½" (75.6cm)
1 yd = 36" (86cm)

Decimal to Inch

.125 = ⅛" (0.3cm)
.25 = ¼" (0.6cm)
.375 = ⅜" (0.9cm)
.50 = ½" (1.2cm)
.625 = ⅝" (1.5cm)
.75 = ¾ (1.8cm)
.875 = ⅞" (2.1cm)
1.0 = 1" (2.4cm)

Estimating the amount of fabric you will need is not a difficult task. After making a quilt or two you will want to be able to estimate your own yardage. You may save money and you won't run out of that favorite fabric only to find that there is not more available.

To begin to learn to estimate yardage you basically need to know how much yardage it takes to cover the bed, and then add about one fourth or 25% to that amount to allow for the seam allowances of the many seams used in the quilt.

Each quilt plan in this book lists the amount of yardage required to make a top. Yardage estimates for the blocks, sashing, setting squares, border and backing are also included.

Estimate the yardage requirements by dividing the total number of different fabrics into the number of yards of fabric required for the quilt size you have chosen. For example, if you are making a king-size quilt that calls for nine yards of fabric for the blocks and you have selected twelve different fabrics, divide 12 into the 9 yards (9÷12= .75 or ¾ yd [64.8cm]). This means you'll need approximately ¾ yard (64.8cm) of each fabric.

Purchase at least ½ yard (43cm) of each fabric. Purchase 1 yard (86cm) each of your favorite fabrics, and 3½ yards (30m) if the fabric will be used in both the quilt and border. If you purchase the border fabric when you select the fabrics for the blocks, set this fabric aside. This will ensure that you will have the long lengths needed when you are ready to cut and sew the borders.

Every quilt design will require a different amount of yardage. The easiest way to begin the estimating process is to use some graph paper and draw a diagram. Add a pocket calculator to help estimate the yardage.

I've included some basic conversion charts—inches to yards and inches to decimals for use with the calculator. The estimates in this book are general and ample. In most cases the estimate is calculated on the use of seven different fabrics. It is very simple to estimate the yards needed if you add or subtract from the number seven. Look at the plan you've selected. If it says that you need 1½ yards (12.9m) of seven fabrics, that is 10½ (90m) yards total. If you change the number from 7 to 9, you must divide 9 into the 10½ total, or 1⅛ yards (9.6m). Use the charts as given for your first quilt, or estimate your own.

Find the plan of the quilt size that you want to make. The yardage estimate is provided for each size of quilt.

Fabric Width

The manufacturers' widths vary, so I refer to 45" fabric as 40"- 42" (105cm) wide. (42" (105cm) is the approximate width of the 45" (108cm) fabric after it has been washed and the selvage edge has been removed).

Grain Line

The cotton fabric threads are woven in two directions, referred to as the grain of the fabric. Lines marked on each pattern indicate which direction to place the pattern—along the lengthwise or crosswise grain lines.

Lengthwise grain is parallel to the selvage, running up and down. Fabric has little, if any, stretch lengthwise. Fabric is usually printed straight along the lengthwise grain.

Crosswise grain is across the width, from selvage to selvage. Fabric stretches somewhat across the grain. Printed fabric is often not printed straight across the grain. The crosswise grain will ease and stretch in the sewing process.

Bias grain is at any angle other than lengthwise or crosswise. True bias is across the crosswise and lengthwise grains at a 45° angle. The bias has a lot of stretch. The longest side of a pattern piece is placed on the lengthwise grain whenever possible. A lengthwise or crosswise grain is preferred on any edge that will be along the outer edge of a block. The lengthwise grain can be used to stop an area from stretching, as it stabilizes a crossgrain or bias seam. Sew a bias edge to a straight edge whenever possible to prevent having a stretched or distorted seam. Avoid a bias edge on an outside edge of a block. If a bias edge ends up at an outside edge, sew a short running stitch by hand ⅛" (0.3cm) in from the edge to stabilize it.

None of the above "rules" can be followed all of the time. Placement of motifs in fabric may be cut off-grain to showcase a print. Just be more careful if the fabric is cut off-grain, as a bias on the outside edge may stretch.

Selvage

The selvage is the lengthwise edge of the fabric where the threads are doubled when woven. It is difficult to hand sew through this thickness so the selvages are removed before sewing. Use a rotary cutter and cut off all of the selvages as soon as the fabric has been washed, and before it is put away or used.

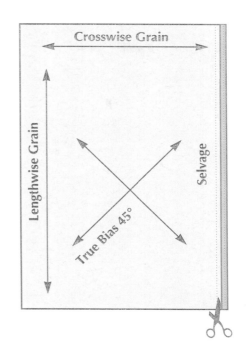

Quilt Plans

Quilt Top Dimensions

Measure the bed with a cloth measuring tape. If the quilt will be covering a pillow, measure over the pillow and into the pillow tuck, tucking the tape as far as you want the pillow tuck to be. Measure the sides of the bed to the edge of where the quilt edge will be. A drop of 13" (31.2cm) from the top edge of the bed will cover most blankets when they are tucked in. The quilt plans in this book include 13" (31.2cm) at the foot and sides, and a pillow tuck of 12" (28cm). If the quilt is to fall to the floor, add the additional distance to the length and width on the plan. If you increase the measurements of the length and width of the quilt, you will need to purchase more fabric than noted in the quilt plan.

Finished Quilt Dimensions

	Mattress Top ▼	13" Drop and a 12" Pillow Tuck		21" Drop (to the floor) and a 12" Pillow Tuck	
		Width ▼	Length ▼	Width ▼	Length ▼
CRIB ➤	23" x 46"	40"	60"	-------	-------
TWIN ➤	39" x 74	65"	99"	84"	107"
FULL ➤	54" x 75"	84"	106"	100"	114"
QUEEN ➤	60" x 80"	90"	112"	106"	120"
KING ➤	72" x 84"	102"	116"	118"	124"

Use these diagrams as reference as to how to measure your bed. The examples shown represent a twin size bed. Adjust the measurements to fit your bed size. Use the following equation of mattress length plus drop, pillow tuck and pillow cover to figure your quilt size.

For example, for a twin size bed:

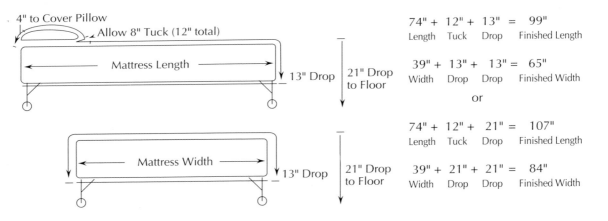

$$74" + 12" + 13" = 99"$$
Length — Tuck — Drop — Finished Length

$$39" + 13" + 13" = 65"$$
Width — Drop — Drop — Finished Width

or

$$74" + 12" + 21" = 107"$$
Length — Tuck — Drop — Finished Length

$$39" + 21" + 21" = 84"$$
Width — Drop — Drop — Finished Width

Whenever possible, place the finished inner top on the bed. Measure the amount you need for the borders. Draw a diagram and estimate the yardage needed. The quilt can shrink as much as 2"- 6" (5-15cm) on all sides (approximately 1" (2.4cm) shrinkage in both width and length to each two square feet), depending on how much quilting is done. Due to this, I have allowed for an average amount of shrinkage in each quilt plan and the yardage estimates. Adjust for the shrinkage lost in quilting if you change the dimensions of your quilt.

Sampler Quilt designed and made by Shirley Gangemi. This theme quilt was made during the Persian Gulf War as a tribute to our sevicemen and women.

Twin Size Quilt

All measurements are for finished size. The requirements include the extra inches needed to allow for the shrinkage due to the quilting. **Add** seam allowance to **all** measurements when cutting. All measurements are approximate.

Finished Quilt Size 66" (W) x 96" (L)
(Includes a 12" pillow tuck +13" drop)

Quilt Size before quilting 72" (W) x 105" (L)

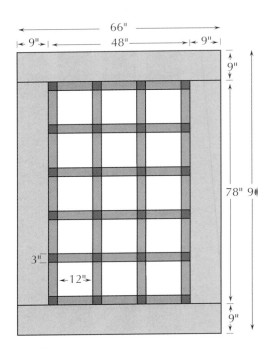

Mattress size	39" (W) x 74" (L)			
Inner top, no border	48" (W) x 78" (L)			
Block size	12" x 12"	15 squares	¾ yd. each of 7 fabrics	5½ yds. total
Sashing fabric	3" x 12"	38 pieces	1 fabric	1½ yds. total
Setting square fabric	3" x 3"	24 pieces	1 fabric	⅜ yd. total
Border fabric L (2)	11" x 82"	4 pieces	1 fabric	3 yds. total
W (2)	11" x 70"	4 pieces	1 fabric	3 yds. total
Backing fabric	72" x 105"	2 lengths 40" wide	1 fabric	6 yds. total
Batting	72" x 105"	1 full sheet, or 6 yds. 45" wide batt		

Bias Binding: Cut 2½" wide, lineal yds. needed: 9 yds.; 1¼ yd. square of 1 fabric
Straight Binding: Eight 40" strips 2½" wide, or ¾ yd. total.

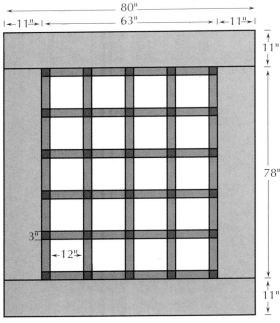

Full (Standard) Size Quilt

All measurements are for finished size. The requirements include the extra inches needed to allow for the shrinkage due to the quilting. **Add** seam allowance to **all** measurements when cutting. All measurements are approximate.

Finished Quilt Size 80" (W) x 100" (L)
(Includes a 12" pillow tuck +13" drop)

Quilt Size before quilting 85" (W) x 105" (L)

Mattress size	54" (W) x 75" (L)			
Inner top, no border	63" (W) x 78" (L)			
Block size	12" x 12"	20 squares	¾ yd. each of 7 fabrics	5½ yds. tot
Sashing fabric	3" x 12"	38 pieces	1 fabric	1½ yds. tot
Setting square fabric	3" x 3"	24 pieces	1 fabric	⅜ yd. total
Border fabric L (2)	13" x 82"	2 pieces	1 fabric	3 yds. total
W (2)	13" x 80"	2 pieces		
Backing fabric	90" x 105"	2 lengths 40" wide	1 fabric	6¼ yds. tot
Batting	90" x 105"	1 full sheet, or 6 yds. 45" wide batt		

Bias Binding: Cut 2½" wide, lineal yds. needed: 10½ yds.; 1¼ yd. square of 1 fab
Straight Binding: Ten 40" strips 2½" wide, or ¾ yd. total.

Queen Size Quilt

All measurements are for finished size. The requirements include the extra inches needed to allow for the shrinkage due to the quilting. **Add** seam allowance to **all** measurements when cutting. All measurements are approximate.

Finished Quilt Size 86" (W) x 105" (L)
(Includes a 12" pillow tuck +13" drop)

Quilt Size before quilting 90" (W) x 110" (L)

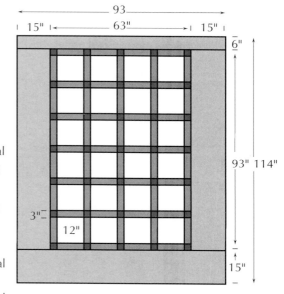

Mattress size	60" x 80"			
Inner top, no border	63" (W) x 93" (L)			
Block size	12" x 12"	24 squares	1½ yds. ea.	
		of 7 fabrics	10½ yds. total	
Sashing fabric	3" x 12"	35 pieces	1 fabric	1½ yds.total
Setting square fabric	3" x 3"	35 pieces	1 fabric	½ yd. total
Border fabric Top	(1) 6" x 93"	1 piece		
Bottom	(1) 15" x 93"	1 piece	1 fabric	3 yds. total
Sides	(2) 15" x 93"	2 pieces		
Backing fabric*	96" x 114"	3 lengths		
	40" wide	1 fabric		10 yds. total
Batting	96" x 114"	1 full sheet, or		
	3 114" lengths	of 45" batt		10 yds. total

*There will be 2 pieces 114" x 30" wide of leftover backing fabric—if you are purchasing the back when you buy the fabric for the front, plan ahead and use some of this leftover fabric in the quilt (approximately 1½ sq. yards will be left over to use).

King Size Quilt

All measurements are for finished size. The requirements include the extra inches needed to allow for the shrinkage due to the quilting. **Add** seam allowance to **all** measurements when cutting. All measurements are approximate.

Finished Quilt Size 98" (W) x 109" (L)
(Includes a 12" pillow tuck +13" drop)

Quilt Size before quilting 104" (W) x 114" (L)

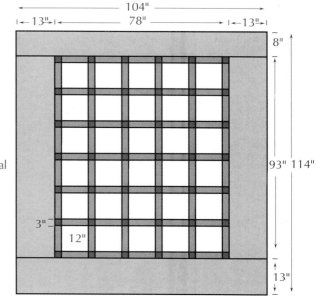

Mattress size	72" x 84"			
Inner top, no border	78" (W) x 93" (L)			
Block size	12" x 12"	30 squares	1½ yd. ea.	
		of 7 fabrics	10½ yds. total	
Sashing fabric	3" x 12"	42 pieces	1 fabric	2 yds.total
Setting square fabric	3" x 3"	42 pieces	1 fabric	⅜ yd. total
Border fabric Top	(1) 8" x 103"	1 piece		
Bottom	(1) 13" x103"	1 piece	1 fabric	3 yds. total
Sides	(2) 13" x 94"	2 pieces		
Backing fabric	104" x 114"	2 lengths		
		40" wide	1 fabric	10½ yds.
Batting	104" x 114"	1 full sheet, or		
		3 120" lengths	of 45" batt	10½ yds. total

Fabric Selection

Perhaps the most exciting step of making a Sampler Quilt is the fabric selection. However, choosing fabrics can seem to be an overwhelming task for the beginner. How do you choose fabrics from the vast array available? How do you choose that first fabric? I will give you a few ideas about prints, color, texture, and style to guide you through the selection process.

I have suggested the use of seven fabrics to make the entire Sampler. This number is not set in stone; it is just a guideline to get you started and to help with estimating the yardage. If you find more fabrics that you cannot possibly live without, by all means add them—you may feel that you need more contrast or variety. Students have used over twenty coordinated prints and solids with great success. I made a Sampler using over 125 fabrics.

Seven fabrics are suggested to get you started. Use as few or as many fabrics as you like, adjusting the total amount of yardage required for the quilt size that you have chosen. When your selection is complete, it will be so well coordinated that you will literally be able to pull any one fabric out of a bag and use that one with any other fabric in the selection, and they will work well together.

Occasionally you may want to add more fabrics after you've begun the blocks. Don't hesitate to add a fabric or two if you see some new ones that you just can't do without.

We are fortunate to have hundreds of beautiful prints available for us to use in quilts. Many textile designers, myself included, are creating designs specifically for the quilter. (See page 30 for the Diana Leone collection from Kona Bay Fabrics.) Most manufacturers coordinate within their own lines and do not intend you to combine their fabrics with fabrics from another manufacturer. My line is designed to be used with all of your favorite fabrics. A variety selected from different manufacturers will rarely exactly match each other. Let the prints blend, and if the colors are close, accept that they will never match. After they have been sewn together, the fabrics will change with age, washing, and exposure to light.

The fabric you choose for the quilt should be the best you can afford. A lot of time, money and effort are put into the quilt, and the fabric should be worthy of this time and effort. Use 100% cotton for quiltmaking. "Even-weave" or standard print cloth is the base cloth for prints and solids. The thread count is between 68 and 88 threads per square inch. Any fabric with a lesser thread count will shrink and increase the possibility of bearding. Sheets are not recommended for use in quilting or as backing for quilts, as the threads are woven too closely, they are difficult to quilt through, and they have a tendency to "pill."

Be creative in your fabric selection. You are the one making the choices, and the sky is the limit. You should like your fabric selection so much that you can hardly wait to begin your quilt.

The rest of this chapter provides guidelines for choosing fabric. You do not need to master this material. You can simply choose seven or more fabrics that appeal to you and begin.

TIP
It takes as long to make something of value out of good cloth as it does out of poor cloth. Use the best quality you can afford.

A few of the solids available from the hundreds that are manufactured.

Textured prints of low contrast may be used as solids.

Solid Fabric

Solid or plain 100% cotton fabric is made of the same cloth that is used to produce the cotton prints we use in quilts. Solid fabrics are available in over 600 different hues, tints, tones and shades. Either side of a solid fabric may be used.

Print Fabric

In the broadest sense of the word, a print is anything from the small microdot to a very large repeat. I consider florals, plaids, stripes, geometrics—anything that is not a solid—to be prints. Printed fabric is imprinted on one side, creating a "right" and a "wrong" side. The wrong side may sometimes be used as a lighter value of the same color. Plaids and stripes may be printed or woven. Many tone-on-tone prints can be used as a solid color. Printed fabric creates texture.

Value of Fabric

When you look at a quilt, the first thing that you see is its color. The second image that you see will be the patterns created from the contrast in value of the colors used. Learning to use value, color and design can be explored through the process of making the Sampler Quilt.

Value is the relationship of light to dark. Value is relative—a medium fabric in one group may appear light in another set. Learning to see the value of a fabric will help you to determine its placement. Whether combining prints or solids, you'll want to develop the contrast of value within the pattern of the block.

Light values come forward. Use light values in small amounts as accents, or to feature a part of a design. Lighter values are also used as the background for appliquéd blocks to contrast with the appliqué design.

Dark values recede. Dark fabrics may be used also as the background or as accents. Medium values produce an overall muted appearance. Sixty percent of all prints and solids are of a medium value. If you use mostly medium values the design of the patterns becomes lost. Use medium values in combination with light and dark values to develop the contrast needed to bring out the design elements of the patterns.

Solid fabrics provide color and value, but prints provide color, value and texture. How you combine these elements—the prints or solids you choose to make the Sampler Quilt—is what creates its style, mood and appeal.

As an exercise, look at your fabrics from a distance. Separate the fabrics into light, medium and darks. Glue little pieces of fabrics to one of the line drawings on the pattern pages. This will help you to see the contrast and develop the pattern.

Use the diagram on the next page to practice seeing value.

A monochromatic selection with a balance of value, print size and texture.

A selection showing fabrics very similar in value.

The same selection is enhanced when value contrasts are added. The added colors add the accents and value contrast.

A value scale from light to dark, using achromatic and polychromatic fabrics.

	Light				Medium				Dark
Gray Scale									
Gray Scale Cut and paste solids or prints white to black.									
Monochromatic Cut and paste solids or prints of one color (e.g. all blues).									
Polychromatic Cut and paste solids or prints of many different colors.									

Use this chart to practice seeing the value of the fabrics. Find the similar value of your fabrics to the gray value. Cut and paste the fabrics onto the chart. Use prints and/or solids.

Template
1⅛" x ⅝"
Cut 1

Sampler Quilt designed and made by Bonnie Minardi.

Prints as Color

To determine a print's color, stand back a few feet and squint. What is the dominant color? For example, a fabric viewed up close is predominantly pale blue with tiny pink flowers, but when viewed from a few feet away, it may appear as a soft lavender or light blue. Use the print as a guide to help you begin the selection. I've found that people tend to look at a printed fabric and see each individual color, instead of the overall color and value. It is better to see the overall color in the fabric than to try to match each different color exactly. You can manipulate or blend the colors in the fabric to become what you want or need the color to become. Read about "The Blender", page 34.

You may love a particular fabric that doesn't include all of the colors that you want to use. You can still make it work for you. Look at the fabric, and then look at the color wheel.

The following three harmonies are the most used by fabric designers. Using any one of these harmonies in a quilt will produce a beautiful result.

Find the dominant color in the fabric, then find that color on the wheel. See if the colors that you want to use are within an analogous, complementary or split complementary harmony. Select that harmony and use it as an aid in coordinating the fabric selection.

Analogous

Analogous colors.

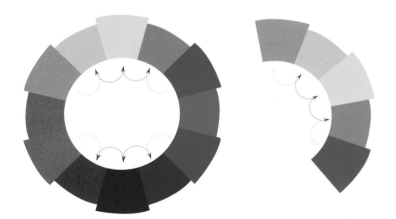

Analogous colors are adjacent on the color wheel. The "adjacents" will include a primary or secondary color. Analogous colors are always pleasing to the eye, easy to work with, and produce a harmonious effect. Analogous colors are either warm or cool combinations, not a combination of both. Add the colors on either side of the three adjacents to enhance the combination. The frontispiece quilt is a good example of the use of analogous colors.

"Land of the Free—Home of the Brave" pictorial Sampler Quilt, made of 30 blocks from over 300 solid fabrics. Hand pieced by Diana Leone, © 1987. Hand quilted by Cathy Risso.

Complementary

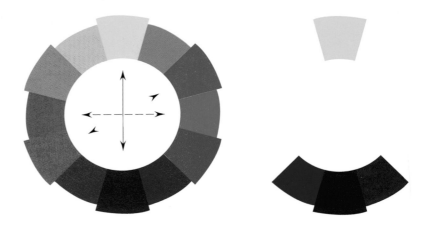

Complementary colors are opposite each other on the color wheel. Opposite colors complement each other and excite the eye. Complementary colors always include a warm and a cool color. Use the direct opposites and the colors next to the opposites to form an exciting and pleasing color scheme.

Split Complementary

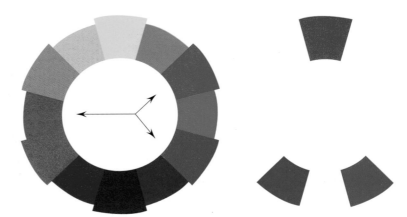

Split complements are harmonious relationships combining one color and the two colors next to its opposite on the color wheel. The split complementary combination includes a warm/cool combination. Use the adjacent colors to add the pleasing combination of the analogous look.

Split complements are common color combinations in multi-print fabrics. These combinations produce exciting effects, and integrate a wider variety of harmonious colors.

"Amish Legacy" Sampler Quilt, pieced and quilted by Virginia Schnalle. Note the use of the yellow accents, which move the eye around the quilt top.

Style and Mood

Look at old quilts and see how the prints affect the style of the quilt. To develop a traditional style, use a variety of small prints and muted colors of low-value contrast. Plaids, stripes and novelty prints were used in the early 1900s. Soft pastels combined with novelty prints create a 1930s look. An Amish style combines deep, rich, dark solid fabrics.

A contemporary style is created by using large abstract prints and bold color with high contrasting values. Contemporary is whatever is popular today—and in the 1990s, it's clear colors, large florals, abstracts and high value contrast—almost anything goes.

Solid fabrics have been used throughout the history of quiltmaking. Solid fabrics may be used by themselves or combined with prints to create a traditional or contemporary style.

Mood is the feeling you want the viewer to "feel." Mood is determined by color. Pastels appear soft and refreshing. Reds and yellows generate a warm feeling and activity. Blues and greens are cool and restful.

Rich earth tones and small textured prints produce an 1890's style.

The same prints with the large floral added produces an Oriental style.

Amish Sampler, 1989. Designed by Diana Leone. Pieced and hand quilted by Doris Olds. Note the small pieces of green fabric, which cause the eye to move around the quilt.

"Wheels". Pattern definition is produced by the use of high contrast in the value of the fabric and contrast in the scale of the print.

Print Texture

Texture is the surface design that the print creates. All prints have texture. The texture is created by the contrast of value of the print to the print's background color. A white print on a very light blue background has less texture (value contrast) than a light blue print on a dark blue background.

Using a balance of small, medium and large prints of different texture, values and/or colors is much more interesting than using three prints of the same size, texture, value and color.

A fabric with designs measuring 3" to 4" (7.5 - 9.5cm) or larger with a high value contrast within the print will add a sparkle and interest to your quilt that can be achieved in no other way. I particularly enjoy using large florals, novelties, geometrics, stripes or paisleys, as they can add spatial dimension, movement and openness to the work. If you try a large print, it can become an important learning tool, and a springboard to more contemporary work. Large prints can be used at random, or with careful planning. To maintain a pattern definition when using a large print, use a strong value contrast fabric in the background, or the large print fabric will become lost into the value of the background.

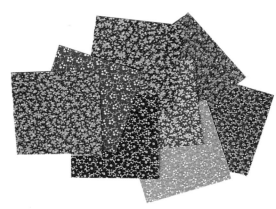

Small prints — low contrast.

Medium size—high contrast.

High contrast—novelty prints.

High contrast—textured prints.

Contemporary Log Cabin quilt pieced and hand quilted by Sondra Rudey.

Aloha, Mahalo, 1990, by Diana Leone. A four-patch designed on a computer. Over 200 different Hawaiian prints were used in this quilt. The theme is a thanksgiving to Hawaii for the memories, love and friendship found in the Islands. The appliqués are hand sewn, using large prints and the Broderie Perse, or "needleturn" technique.

Hurt no Living Thing, pieced and quilted by Kathy Galos, 1991.

Basic Guidelines to Follow in Fabric Selection

1. Select the "blender"— the one print that includes all of the colors that you want to use.

2. Select a variety of light, medium, and dark values in prints and solids to coordinate with the blender.

3. Select a variety of small, medium and large scale prints.

4. Use all prints or all solids, or any combination of the two.

The "Blender"

Begin by finding that one fabric you like most. The "blender" may include only lights and darks in one color family (monochromatic) or it may include all of the colors you like and want to coordinate. This blender print will help you to select the coordinating prints and solids. For example, you've selected a blue print with lavender and a touch of yellows and greens. You want to bring out the blues and purples in the fabric to match the room where the quilt will be placed. Select fabrics that you like and place them next to the blender fabric. See how much you can change or adapt the colors to become a combination that you like.

When you look at the blender print fabric, you may see three or four colors in it. You will probably try to feature or exactly match some particular color in the print. Rather than exactly matching any particular color in the print, stand back and look at the whole piece. What do you really see? Do you see a blending of colors? Do you see one color more than the others? Do you see the color that you want to bring out and feature?

After you have found the blender, choose six more fabrics to coordinate with it. Contrasting the value (the lightness or darkness of the color) to the print is more important than finding an exact color match to a color in the print. An exact color match will blend into the print and become lost. The pattern of the block is defined only when there is a contrast in color or value.

The last fabric should be the accent. It may be an opposite, a bright, a light, or a very dark fabric. The accent should be used in a smaller amount. On occasion, after coordinating the fabrics with the blender, you may decide not to use the original fabric. The selection of other fabrics you have chosen will be beautifully coordinated, and you may decide that you don't even need the original blender fabric.

Preparing the Fabrics

All fabrics should be washed before using them in a quilt. Before washing, cut off the selvages and cut a small triangle off of each corner to stop the edges from raveling while washing. Washing shrinks the fabric and removes most excess dye and sizing. The fabric needs only to get wet and be dried; it does not need to go through the full wash cycle. Use ¼ cup of phosphorous- and bleach-free, mild soap in a full wash load. I recommend Easy Wash™ or Orvus™ soap.

Fabric Dyes

The cloth used in the quilt industry prints well, accepts dyes and stands up to the test of time. Because of our environmental laws, USA print plants cannot use strong dye fixatives, as they pollute the waterways. Domestic printed cotton fabrics may fade and expel more excess dye than cloth manufactured in Europe or the countries of the Pacific Rim.

Dye Run Test

Fabric can be tested to see if the dye is stable. Some dark fabrics may have excess surface dye that is removed when the fabric is washed. If there is any question, rub the cloth on a piece of white cotton cloth. If the fabric's color shows on the white fabric, treat it as follows to release and/or set the excess dye:

1. Place the fabric in a dishpan filled with hot water mixed with 2 cups of white vinegar and ½ cup of borax or washing soda.

2. Let the fabric sit in the solution for at least two hours, then rinse in cold water until the water runs clear.

On occasion a dye will run excessively. If the dye still runs after three or four rinsings, you might want to discard this particular fabric. The fabric may be "crocking." In this case, the dye was not properly set and the dye may never stop running. Discontinue the use of this fabric.

Fabric Fading

Domestically dyed and printed fabric may fade when exposed to sunlight or indoor lighting. More fading occurs on dark fabrics, particularly the dark blues, dark reds and browns.

I had a quilt on my bed that was made of dark blues, dark greens and burgundy. The side next to the light from the north window faded to a point where the prints were unrecognizable. There is really nothing that can be done to stop this when using domestic cottons, except to avoid using dark fabrics, or accept the fading as the patina that occurs with aging.

TIPS

Place the fabric in the dryer on a warm/cool temperature. Heat will set wrinkles in the cloth. Place a large dry towel in the dryer with the fabric. The fabric will dry very quickly because the towel absorbs the moisture and also acts as a buffer to help prevent the fabric from twisting.

Remove the fabric before it is completely dry, possibly in as few as 5-10 minutes. Smooth it with your hands. Press while slightly damp.

To keep fabric wrinkle-free after ironing, hang the fabric from a pants hanger by the selvage edge.

Use spray starch on the fabric before cutting. The fabric will be easier to cut with the added crispness.

Getting Started

There are many methods of piecing a quilt. The quilt top may be sewn by hand or machine, or a combination of both. The pieces of the blocks are marked, cut and sewn together. The inner top is sewn and the borders are added.

The methods presented here ensure that you will learn traditional and accurate techniques to make templates, and to mark and cut the fabric; give you suggestions for placing or pinning the fabric pieces for a block onto a flannel square to provide portability for your work; and teach you how to pin the pieces together with fine pins, using the dot-to-dot method, for optimum piecing results.

You will use template plastic and trace the full-size patterns from the book. The fabrics are marked and cut using scissors, or with some experience, a rotary cutter.

Instructions are given on how to sew by hand or machine, using cotton thread. A medium gray or beige thread is a good neutral choice for the majority of piecing.

Machine pieced seams should be pressed to one side (toward the darker fabric) to ensure the strongest seam, or pressed open to avoid bulky seam crossings. Hand-pieced seams are generally pressed to one side—usually toward the darker fabric, as this makes a hand-pieced seam stronger and provides an area with no seam, which is easier to hand quilt.

Selecting the Patterns and Beginning the Blocks

There are thirty-six block patterns in this book—all are full size and ready to trace. Choose any pattern to begin with, depending on your experience level. All of the patterns are labeled as to their complexity: 🪡 easy, 🪡🪡 average, 🪡🪡🪡 intermediate, 🪡🪡🪡🪡 complex.

Patchwork blocks are made by making a template, marking the fabric on the wrong side, and cutting out the pieces. The pieces are sewn together by hand or machine. The smallest pieces are sewn together first. When these pieces are sewn together they become units. The units are sewed together into rows. The rows are then sewed together to form a 12" (28cm) finished block (12½" [30cm] unfinished).

Appliqué blocks are constructed by hand. Appliqué is worked on the front of the block. The design is marked on the right side of the background fabric. After the appliqué fabric pieces are cut, they are aligned with the placement lines marked on the background fabric, and then basted in place. The pieces are sewed by hand to the background fabric, using a blind hem stitch.

Making the Templates

Templates, cut from thin, rigid plastic sheets, are the guides used to trace the pattern pieces onto the fabric. Thin cardboard may be used for templates, but with use the cardboard edges will become worn down, causing inaccurate marking and piecing. Plastic templates are accurate, long-lasting, and can be reused indefinitely. Six 8½" x 11" (20.4 x 26.4cm) sheets of template plastic are needed to cut all of the templates for the thirty-six patterns in this book. You can use either gridded or non-gridded plastic made for this purpose.

Patchwork Block

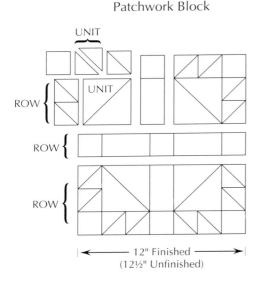

12" Finished
(12½" Unfinished)

Appliqué Block

There are two different ways to make templates. Method I does not include the seam allowance in the template; Method II includes the seam allowance in the template. I find that I need a marked line to cut on and a second line to sew on, so I use Method II and mark both the sewing line and the cutting line.

Preparing your fabric pieces for perfect sewing begins with the accuracy of the template you use. A fine line Sharpie™ or any other permanent felt marker and a good pair of sharp scissors are necessary tools to use to mark and cut an accurate template. Carefully cut templates are an important step to accurately pieced blocks.

Each different part of a block requires a template; each pattern lists the number of different templates to cut. You will notice that the templates in many of the patterns are the same size—some templates may be used for more than one block. Rather than make another identical template, label each template as to its use and interchangeability. Write any other information you might need about the template (name of the block, size, how many to cut, page number, etc.) on a label and adhere it to each template.

Store the templates for each pattern in a different envelope. Write the name of the block and draw a small picture of the pattern on the envelope.

Some templates may be used for marking reverse shapes. These pieces are indicated with an (R) on the pattern pages. Mark these templates clearly in order to know which side of the template should be face up or down on the fabric.

I suggest that you make a block using Method I, and then make a block using Method II to see which method you prefer. You will quickly discover which method you like to use. You may use both methods in one project. Use the templates that include the seam allowance for curved seams.

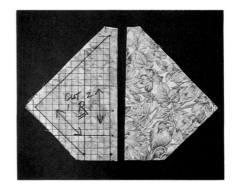

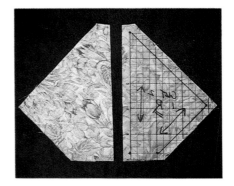

Reverse Shapes

Method I
The Template without the ¼" Seam Allowance

This technique is used for hand or machine piecing, when a marked sewing guideline is desired. The ¼" (0.6cm) seam allowance is added with a ruler or "by eye" when the piece is cut from the fabric. Place a strip of ¼" tape ¼" away from one edge of your ruler, as shown at left. Always use the same edge for all of your marking.

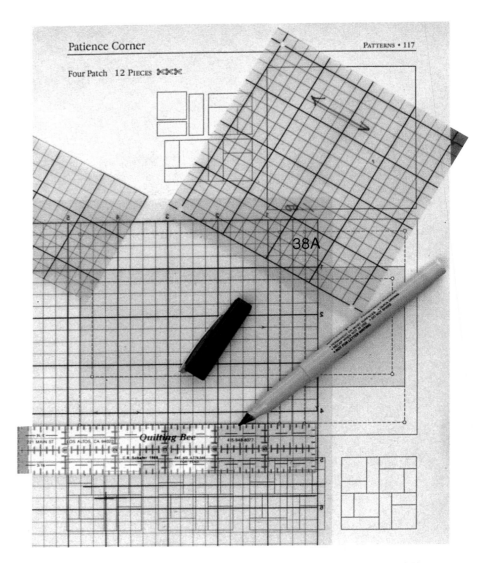

Choose a block pattern. Patience Corner (page 123) is an easy one to use.

Place a sheet of template plastic over the pattern piece.

Place a clear ruler next to the inside line (seam line) on the pattern.

Trace the line onto the plastic with a permanent fine tip felt marker or pencil.

Mark the match marks and grain line onto the plastic as indicated on the pattern.

Using a pair of sharp scissors, carefully cut the plastic on the marked cutting line.

To check for accuracy, place the completed template over the pattern in the book. If your template is smaller or larger than the pattern, make a new template. If your templates are accurate, you are ready to mark and cut the fabric.

The seam allowance will be added when the fabric is cut.

Method II: "Dot-to-Dot"
The Template with the ¼" Seam Allowance

This technique is used for hand or machine piecing. The ¼" (0.6cm) seam allowance is included in the template. The corners and where seam lines cross or converge are marked with a dot to accurately match and pin the corresponding seam lines. These corners are indicated on the template with a dot—hence "dot-to-dot" pinning and piecing. These dots, or match marks, are key to successful piecing.

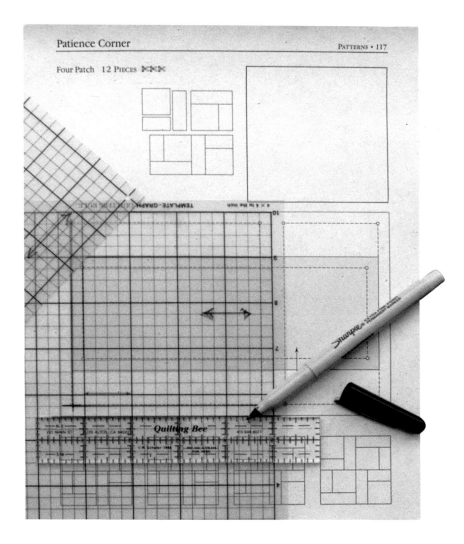

Choose a block pattern. Patience Corner (page 123) is an easy one to start with.

Place the template plastic over the pattern piece. Place the ruler along the outside line (cutting line) of the pattern. Use a fine permanent felt-tip marker and trace the line. Mark close to the ruler's edge in order to trace the pattern as accurately as possible.

Mark the dots and any other match marks indicated on the pattern onto the plastic.

Transfer the grain line onto the plastic as indicated on the pattern.

Using a pair of sharp scissors, carefully cut the plastic on the marked cutting line.

Punch a small hole through the plastic at each marked dot. Use a ¹⁄₁₆" or ⅛" (1.5mm - 0.3cm) hole punch or a size #3 large, sharp yarn darner needle.

To check for accuracy, place the completed template over the pattern in the book. If your template is smaller or larger than the pattern, or if the dots do not align, make a new template. If your templates are accurate, you are ready to mark and cut the fabric.

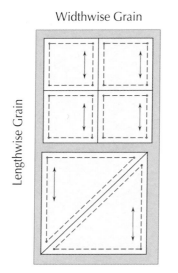

Widthwise Grain

Lengthwise Grain

Marking the Fabric

Use a sandpaper-covered marking board or "lap board" to mark the fabric pieces. The sandpaper keeps the fabric from slipping while it is being marked. Follow instructions for preparing fabric—cut off selvages, wash, dry, and press. Place the fabric on the sandpaper-covered marking board, right side down for patchwork, right side up for appliqué.

Whenever possible, place the longest edge of the template on the lengthwise grain of the fabric. When two or more of the same piece are needed, place the template on the fabric and mark common cutting lines. Use a different colored pen to mark reverse repeats. Use different colored pens when using the same template for a different selected printed design.

When a print design or a directional print is featured, it may not be possible to avoid a bias grain on the outside edge of a block. Sew a row of stay-stitching ³⁄₁₆" (4.5mm) or ¼" (0.6cm) from the edge to stabilize. Sew the stabilizing stitches by hand, being careful not to stretch the fabric.

Place the template on the fabric, aligning the template grain lines with the fabric grain line (as indicated on the template).

Mark around the template's edge with any sharp pencil that will show on the fabric. Mark very close to the edge of the template.

Mark the dots and/or any other match marks as indicated on the template.

In order to prevent the tip of the pencil from pulling the fabric, which may cause distortion of the lines, hold your marking tool at a slight angle when marking around the template.

Remove the template. Place a clear 6" (15cm) ruler next to the dots and connect them. This creates the sewing line.

To add the ¼" (0.6cm) seam allowance for Method II, align the edge of a clear ruler ¼" (0.6cm) outside of the marked pattern line, and draw the cutting line. As you gain more experience, you will be able to gauge the ¼" (0.6cm) distance without a ruler.

Cutting the Fabric with Scissors

The scissors used to cut the fabric are the single most important tool you will use. Use scissors with sharp, well-balanced blades. The Gingher® G7 or G8 are quality scissors. I prefer the 7" scissors, as they are smaller and fit a smaller hand.

Cut the fabric—do not tear the pieces. Torn edges waste fabric and pull threads, resulting in a weakened edge in an already narrow seam allowance.

Scissors lift the edge of the fabric while cutting, making it easy to cut crooked, inaccurate pieces. Therefore, it may be easier to hold the fabric in one hand and cut carefully along the marked line with the other hand. If the fabric is cut crooked, mark and cut another piece to replace it.

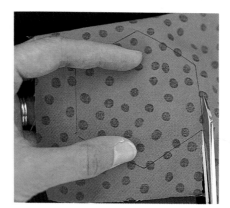

The Rotary Cutter, Cutting Guide/Ruler and Mat

The rotary cutter, cutting guide and self-healing vinyl mat are great tools for the quilter to use. Single or multiple layers of fabric can be cut quickly and accurately with these tools. I do not always recommend the use of these tools to beginners because it is important to learn traditional marking and cutting methods first. As you progress, you will find that these tools will be worth the investment, and you will quickly get your money's worth in the time saved and the fast and accurate cutting of the fabric.

The ideal workspace: a cutting area on a table that you can walk around.

The rotary cutter is a sharp round cutting wheel on a handle. The wheel is rolled on the cutting surface, next to a rigid plastic cutting guide, producing an accurate cut. A self-healing vinyl cutting mat is necessary because the sharp blade will mar any other surface and dull the blade. There are many brands of self-healing mats; some are more long-lasting than others. See the "Supplies and Materials" section. Cutting guides or rulers made of rigid, $1/16$" (1.5mm) thick plastic are used with the rotary cutter. I recommend a 6" x 24" cutting guide. A plastic C-Thru™ ruler is too soft to use, and a metal edged ruler may damage the rotary blade.

The rotary cutter and cutting guide will cut very accurately and save time. Use the rotary cutter to cut off selvages, and to cut the pieces and the sashing strips and borders as described below. The large rotary cutter enables you to cut from one to six layers. Single layers of small pieces are easily cut with the rotary cutter and specialized rectangular cutting guides. With practice, you can learn to use the cutter to cut single or multiple shapes using cutting guides with 45°, 60°, or 90° angles marked on them. Purchase a 6" or 12" square marked with 30°, 60°, or 90° angles. Practice cutting pieces for a block. See Bibliography for additional information.

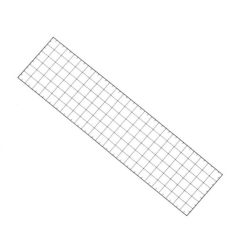

TIP

Always slide the safety cover over the blade when not in use. The blade is very sharp— use the cutter carefully. Be sure to keep the cutter out of the reach of children.

To safely make the first cut, leave the safety cover closed over the blade. Push firmly to release the blade and make the cut.

Using the Rotary Cutter

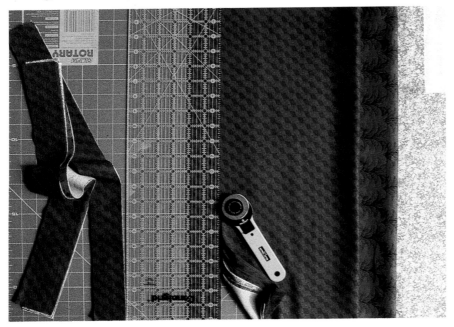

TIP

When folding the fabric in half, be sure that there are no ripples or pulls along the fold. Grasp the fabric along the fold and let it fall straight. Fold the fabric into fourths for faster cutting.

Note: these are right-handed instructions.

Practice cutting a 2" (5cm) strip from a ¼ yard (0.25m) width of fabric.

Fold the fabric in half, selvage to selvage. When folding the fabric in half, be sure that there are no ripples or pulls along the fold. Grasp the fabric along the fold and let it fall straight. The fabric may be folded in half again to save room. When cutting more than one fabric, it is best to fold the fabrics only one time. Place the folded edge toward you on the cutting mat. The fabric to be cut is to the right of the cutting guide.

Place the cutting guide over the left-hand raw edges of the fabric, covering about 1" (2.4cm), or enough to cover the uneven edges.

Align the lines on the cutting guide with lines on the mat and the folded edge of the fabric.

Place your left hand firmly on the cutting guide, near the bottom edge, next to the cutting blade.

Place the blade of the rotary cutter next to the guide's edge, parallel to the hand holding the cutting guide. Press firmly on both the guide and the blade as you roll the cutter next to the guide. Cut away from the body, from the edge closest to you to the top. Cut so firmly that it feels as though you might be cutting through the mat.

Lift the left hand and move it up the guide, holding the guide firmly in place next to the blade as the blade is pushed up along the cutting guide. Cut off the 1" (2.4cm) of excess along the left edge to remove the uneven edges.

Do not cut back and forth or from top to bottom.

Move the cutting guide to the right, 2" (5cm) or the width needed (including the seam allowances) and cut a strip. Check to be sure that the strip is straight.

If it is not, re-cut it.

Cut a few more strips for practice.

Sampler Quilt designed and made by Sylvia Pressacco, 1991.

Piecing

Tips for Accurate Piecing

- Use sharp marking tools
- Mark precisely
- Make accurate templates
- Sew accurately
- Measure carefully and often
- Re-sew if necessary

The standard seam allowance used in patchwork is ¼" (0.6cm). This narrow seam is used so that there is less bulk behind the top. The seam allowance is usually pressed to one side when piecing by hand or machine. The seam may also be pressed to one side or pressed open when piecing by machine. It is easier to quilt next to the edge of the seam or on the side of the seam opposite the seam allowance. It is difficult to quilt through the extra layers of the seam allowance.

If the seam is to become a butted seam, or when two or more seams align and the seams are pressed away from each other, sew from dot to dot, or corner to corner. If the seam will be sewn across by another continuous seam, as in sashings or non-butted seams, sew from edge to edge.

Decide whether to hand or machine piece the blocks. You may do both in one quilt. It is more important that the blocks come out the right size than how it is pieced. Use a ruler and/or use master templates to continually measure the seams, units, rows, and finished blocks.

Keeping Track of the Pieces

A flannel square provides a portable base that keeps the loose pieces in the proper order and ready to sew. I always have some small hand project with me to work on. When I'm making blocks, I pin the pieces to flannel, roll it up and take the block with me wherever I go. I never mind a wait; I always have something to work on and I get a lot done this way.

Cut and hem an 18" (45cm) square of flannel.

Arrange the cut fabric pieces into the same configuration as they will appear in the block.

Pin the pieces to the flannel right side down for patchwork, and right side up for appliqué. Pick up two pieces, sew them together and place them back onto the flannel, keeping the block in order.

Hand Piecing

Supplies

Needles: Sharps or Betweens, size 9 or 10
Thread: 100% cotton or cotton-wrapped polyester
Scissors: Sharp, for fabric cutting
Scissors: Sharp, for plastic cutting
Pins: Short, fine
Plastic: For templates
Pencils: Wax-based
Needle: Darner or ¹/₁₆" hole punch
Fine-point permanent felt marker
Lapboard—Sandpaper-covered marking board
Rotary cutter, mat and cutting guide

The Single Seam

The single seam is hand sewn from "dot to dot", or beginning ¼" (0.6cm) in from one edge and ending ¼" (0.6cm) from the next edge. Beginning and stopping ¼" (0.6cm) from the edge allows the seams to butt together.

The butted seams, when pressed in opposite directions, reduce bulk at the seams' juncture.

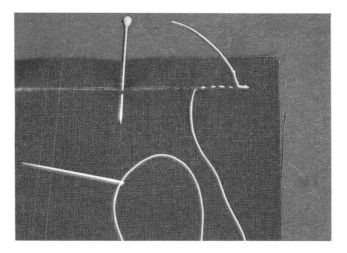

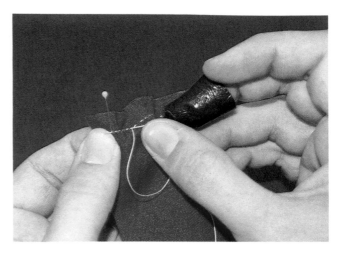

For practice, cut two sets of two 4" (9.6cm) squares of fabric. Mark dots ¼" (0.6cm) from each corner.

Place two pieces with their right sides together. Match corners, dots and edges. Place the first pin through the front dot on the right-hand corner of the fabric, perpendicular to the top of the fabric. Push the pin through to the corresponding marked dot on the piece in back. Push the pin through the pieces, taking a small pin stitch (about two threads' length) into the top fabric. Pin the left-hand dot at the seam line in the same way. Place more pins along the line every inch or so as needed. Pin all pins exactly in the seam line with a small pin stitch.

Thread a Between or Sharp needle with a single strand of cotton thread about 18" (45cm) long. Form a small, single knot on the end that is cut from the spool.

The hand piecing stitch is a simple running stitch. Sew short, straight running stitches. Begin with a backstitch at the right-hand pin if you are right-handed, or the left-hand pin if you are left-handed.

Remove the pin in the dot and backstitch on the dot. Sew forward exactly on the seam line, using a short (6-8 stitches per inch) running stitch.

Check the back line every few stitches. If you are not sewing on the line, remove the needle and align the seam. Sew to the corner dot and backstitch on the dot. Clip the thread.

Finger press the seam allowances to one side, or wait until the block is finished and then press.

The Butted Seam

The butted seam will be used on most hand-pieced blocks and some machine-pieced blocks where two or more seams come together. The seams can be pressed to one side or in a radiating manner, whichever results in the least amount of bulk at the seams' juncture or crossing.

The single seam may become part of a butted seam, or it may be sewn across by another single seam. The single seam is stronger when it is sewn from edge to edge, and it is then sewn across by a longer seam. Sometimes you can plan to sew a seam knowing that it will be sewn across by another seam. Sew from edge to edge unless a butted seam is desired.

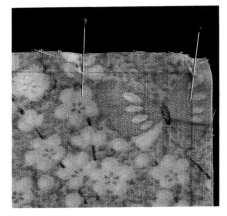

Align two pairs of sewn pieces together.

Pin exactly through the dots or on the seam line.

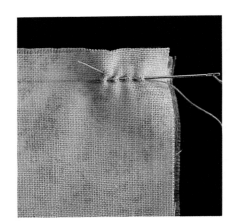

Begin by backstitching at the dot.

Stitch forward to the pin and dot at the butted seam. Check the back to be sure that you are sewing on both seam lines.

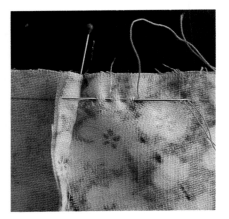

Push the seam allowances away from the seam line. Remove the pin. Backstitch at the dot next to the butted seam.

Slip the needle through the seam allowances. Push the seam allowance back. Backstitch on the dot next to the seam line.

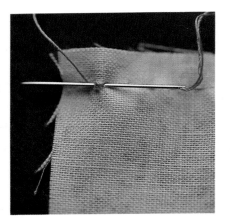

Continue to the dot at the seam's end. End with a backstitch. Clip the threads.

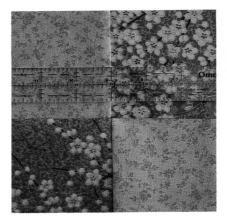

Check the unit for accuracy. Measure the finished unit from seam line to seam line. If it is not the correct size, re-sew as needed.

The Consumed Seam

The seam allowance that is sewn into a seam is used, or consumed. The space between the seam lines must equal the amount needed to produce that part of the block. If the seam is sewn crooked, or into the center area of the patch, the block will become smaller. No matter how carefully you sew, the seams may be crooked, too narrow or too wide. There need to be straight and adequate seam allowances remaining on the unsewn seams for future use.

Once the seam is sewn, measure what it is and what it should be. If it is not correct, fix it now before you compound the error. A 2" (5cm) piece with a 1/16" (1.5mm) error may become an error of 6" (15cm) in a double bed size top.

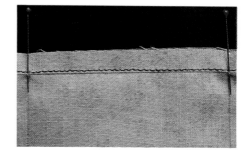

To compensate for the block becoming smaller, sew slightly outside of the marked line or exactly on top of the line. Do not sew into the block.

Set-In Piecing

When piecing a block that requires setting in a square or an angled piece into the corner of the two pieces already sewn, sew from the dot at the center seam out. Do not backstitch into the seam allowances at the corner of the set-in piece. Sew to the edge or backstitch, depending on whether the next seam will cross or butt.

Morning Star (page 120), Attic Windows (page 92), and Peony (page 124) are examples of set-in piecing.

Points

When sewing pointed pieces, the knots on the thead end create an unwanted bulk in the center. To eliminate the bulk, begin sewing ½" in from the dot at the point. Sew to the dot and backstitch. Turn the pieces and sew the seam.

When many points come together, as in stars, gather the points in the center by hand, after all of the joining seams have been sewn. Knot a double strand of strong thread. Use a thread color that matches the top fabrics. Bring the needle from the back to the front at one tip of a point.

Sew through each tip, catching two threads. Sew in a circle. Do not backstitch. Pull on the thread, gathering up the hole in the middle. Slip the needle to the back. Stitch to secure the thread.

Press in a radiating manner.

Curves

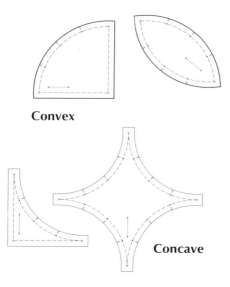

Convex

Concave

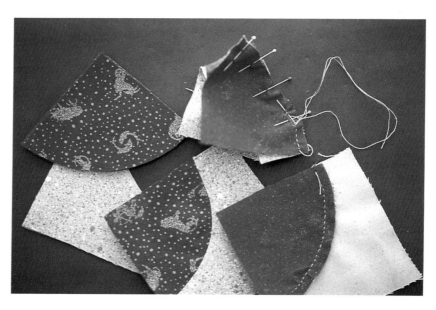

Mark all dots and notch marks shown on the templates to prepare for sewing curves.

When piecing by hand or machine the convex piece is on top. Pin the seam lines at the dots and every ½" (1.2cm) or so. Match the match marks and seam line of the top piece of fabric to the seam line on the bottom piece.

Sew the seam by hand or machine. When sewing by hand, begin and end with a backstitch, and sew from edge to edge. If sewing by machine, sew from edge to edge. For the strongest seam, sew edge to edge when joining curved seams that are crossed by a straight seam.

Sew exactly on the lines, easing the fullness of the convex piece as you sew. Remove the pins as you sew to them. Press the seam away from the convex curve.

Wedge-Shaped Pieces

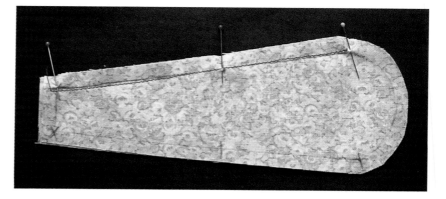

To sew wedge-shaped pieces, stars, Dresden Plates, etc., sew from the narrow end to the wide end. Sew one or two needles' widths inside the seam line to midpoint, then sew on the line. This will ease the center area down.

Machine Piecing

The entire Sampler, except for the hand appliqué, can be machine pieced with perfect results if you cut the pieces accurately, mark and match the dots, pin carefully and take your time when you sew. Machine piecing is faster than hand piecing and very strong. Some quilters use the cut edge of the fabric as the seam guide line. Use Method II when cutting templates for machine piecing. When doing so, you do not need to mark a sewing line, just the dots at the corners and the match marks. The edge of the fabric should be cut ¼" (0.6cm) out from the seam line. Adjust the needle position to ¼" (0.6cm) from the edge of the foot, or place masking tape on the throat plate for the ¼" (0.6cm) guide.

The large open areas in the foot and throat plate were made to accommodate the swing of the needle when zig-zagging, and will cause the seam to slightly draw up or pucker. Use a single hole throat plate, a single hole foot, and a slightly shorter stitch to help make the stitch as perfect as possible. Use a new, sharp sewing machine needle and fine quality cotton thread for machine sewing. A strong stitch length for machine piecing is 12-14 (2.0mm) stitches per inch.

When sewing by machine, do not change machines mid-project, as the width of the feet may vary, causing some blocks to be a different size than the others.

Setting the 1/4" Seam on the Machine

Patchwork piecing is sewn using a ¼" (0.6cm) seam allowance. It is helpful if the foot is ¼" wide or if the needle is adjusted so that it is ¼" (0.6cm) in from the right edge of the foot. Most conventional zig-zag feet on European-made sewing machines are wider than ¼" (0.6cm) from the center needle to the inside, or right edge of the foot. To create a ¼" (0.6cm) seam guide, you can do any of the following:

- On machines with an adjustable needle position, move the needle position to the right until the distance between the needle and the right edge of the foot measures ¼" (0.6cm). Place ¼" tape on the throat plate.

- Some programmable machines can be permanently set to a ¼" (0.6cm) seam.

- Use a Little Foot™, or ask whether a ¼" quilting foot is available for your brand of machine. See "Supplies and Materials", page 10.

The Perfect ¼" Seam Guide

Place a piece of graph paper under the foot. Sew on the ¼" (0.6cm) line from the inside (right) edge. Place a ¼" x 2" long strip of masking tape on the throat plate, along the edge of the paper or ¼" (0.6cm) to the right of the needle.

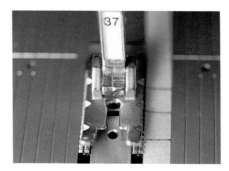

Use "Diana's perfect seam guide". Mark a line on the tape directly across from the needle. Make a second mark ¼" back from the needle and one more ¼" in front of the center mark. When sewing forward, you will know when to stop ¼" from the front edge when the front mark is aligned with the front edge of the fabric. When sewing backwards, you will know to stop ¼" from the back edge when the back mark is aligned with the back edge of the fabric.

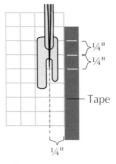
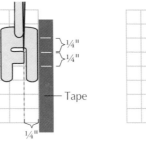
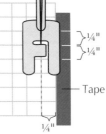

Ideal Presser Foot
Piecing guide marks are indicated on the tape.

¼ Foot
Piecing guide marks are indicated on the tape.

Wide Presser Foot with adjustable needle
Needle is adjusted to ¼" from edge of tape. Piecing guide marks are marked on the tape.

Wide Presser Foot with non-adjustable needle
Edge of tape is slightly under foot and ¼" from needle. Piecing guide marks are indicated on the tape.

The Butted Seam

Use the "dot-to-dot" method to sew the butted seam when you want the least amount of bulk where the seams converge. To form the butted seam, you do not sew into or across the seam allowances. Because you do not sew across the seam, the butted seam allowances will press in any direction, or in a radiating manner, resulting in the least amount of bulk in any one area.

Try the following to practice the technique.

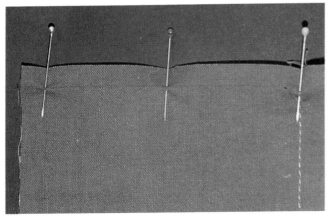

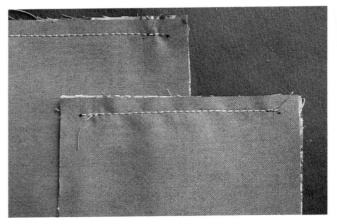

Cut two sets of two 4" (9.6cm) squares of fabric. Mark dots ¼" (0.6cm) from each corner. Pin two squares together. Pin directly into the marked dots, aligning the front and back dots. Exit the pin ¹⁄₃₂" (7.5mm) down or a few threads below the dot, forming a "pin stitch." Pin the dot at the seam's end.

Place the machine needle in the seam line three stitches ahead of the corner pin. Sew backwards exactly to the pin. (This backstitch secures the seam end.) Remove the pin.

Sew forward, removing any pins as you sew to them. Sew to the last pin. Remove the pin. Backstitch three stitches. Lift the pressure foot and remove the fabric. Clip all threads.

Sew a second set of 2" (5cm) squares together.

Press the seams to one direction. Press both sets the same way.

Turn one set in the opposite direction.

Place the pair right sides together. Align and butt the seams together precisely.

Place one pin exactly in the center seam from the front. Exit exactly through the dot on the seam in the back. Take a pin stitch. This pin becomes the "holding pin".

Pin into the dots at the beginning and end of the seam line to hold the pieces together. Pin along the seam line as needed.

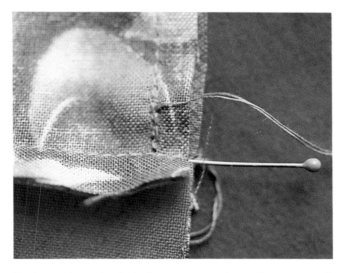

Begin sewing a backstitch at a corner dot and sew toward the butted seam. Hold all the seams away from the needle's path. Remove the pin.

Take two or three backstitches. Raise the pressure foot. Lift the needle by turning the hand wheel to the highest position (this makes it easier to pull the threads loose).

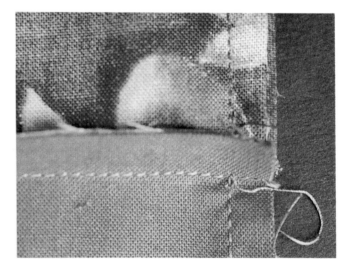

Pull the fabric away from the needle. Pull about 5" (12cm) of thread. Flip all the seams back, or toward the seam you have just sewn. With the seams held back, place the needle into the dot or exactly at the butted seam.

Sew forward to the seam's end dot. Backstitch and clip the threads.

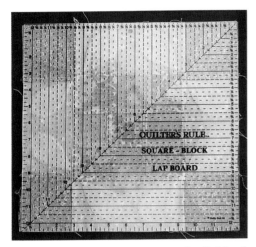

Place the master template over the finished block to check for accuracy.

12" Master Template

To check for accurate marking and sewing of the pieced units, use a master template or a square gridded cutting guide. Cut a template the correct size of the finished block, including seams. All of the blocks in this book, when sewn, measure 12" (28cm) from seam line to seam line, or 12½" (30cm) from edge to edge.

Mark and cut a 12½" (30cm) square template from plastic, or use a 12½" (30cm) square Omnigrid™ or Quilter's Rule™ 12½" (30cm) square printed plexiglas. Place the template over the block. The block should measure 12½" (30cm) from edge to edge. If the block is too small or too large, you may have to take it apart and re-sew some of the seams. The edge of the block may be as much as ¼"- ½" (0.6 - 1.2cm) longer than it should be. Ease this extra ¼"- ½" (0.6 - 1.2cm) of seam by stay stitching by hand ⅛" (0.3cm) from the edge of the block. Pull the stay stitch slightly to ease the seam.

Pressing

Press the seams as you sew, or press the entire block when it is finished. Press the block on the right side first. Turn the block over and press the back, and then press the right side again. Do not push the iron back and forth. For a stronger seam press the seams to one side, usually toward the darker fabric. Press in a circular direction when possible. This method of pressing ensures that the butted seams of two units may be pressed in opposite directions where they meet.

I use the portable, padded June Tailor Pressing Block™. It is next to my machine and easy to use.

Press in a radiating manner. When possible, press toward the darker fabric.

Press in a radiating manner. Press toward the darker fabric.

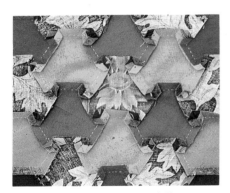

Press as the seams want to fall.

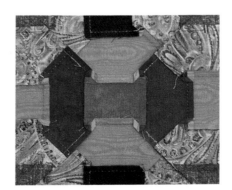

Press as the seams want to fall.

Press toward the convex seam.

Sampler Quilt designed and made by Robin Cole, 1991. Note the narrow border at the top. The inner strip of blue in the border brings the color in the top into the border.

Appliqué

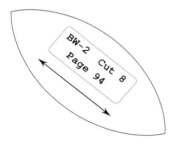

Supplies

Fabric: 100% cotton, washed and pre-shrunk
Thread: 100% cotton or cotton-wrapped polyester
Needles: Sharps, Size 8, 9, 10
Pins: 1" fine
Scissors: Small, sharp scissors for clipping
              Large scissors for cutting large pieces of fabric
              Extra pair of sharp scissors for template and paper cutting
Template plastic—Clear or gridded
Lapboard—Sandpaper-covered marking board
Thimble
Needle threader
Pencils
Pencil Sharpener

Appliqué means to lay on, or to apply one or more pieces of fabric (the appliqué) to the front or right side of another piece of fabric (the background). The appliqué piece is usually a curvilinear form. I find the process of hand appliqué to be as rewarding, if not more so, than patchwork. I enjoy the flexibility and the beauty of appliqué, as well as the ease of having a portable block with the pieces basted in place and ready to work on wherever I am.

Of the many methods of appliqué, I am including two of the easiest and most traditional: the pinch and needleturn and basted edge methods. There are many more methods which you may want to learn after you learn these two traditional techniques. Basically, you will decide if the edges of the pieces need to be turned under and basted before the appliqué is sewed to the background fabric, or if you will turn the edges under as you sew. The blind hem stitch is used for both methods. There are six patterns in this book which use the appliqué techniques: Bridal Wreath, Dresden Plate, Grandmother's Fan, Honey Bee, Iris, and Peony.

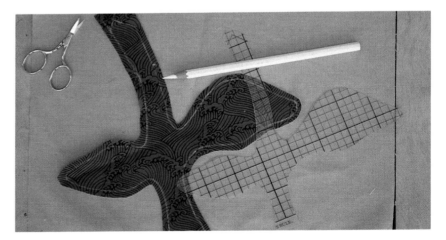

Templates

Each appliqué piece requires a template. The appliqué templates are cut to the size of the finished appliqué pieces. The solid line on the patterns is the template cutting line. The patterns do not include the seam allowance. The scant 3/16" (4.5mm) seam allowance is added by eye when the fabric piece is cut. The templates are made by placing a sheet of template plastic over the pattern pieces in the book and tracing the shape.

The Background Square

In order for the appliqué design to be seen against the background, select a background fabric that contrasts in color or in value with the appliqué pieces. I suggest using a texture print such as a white-on-white print or a one value tone-on-tone print in place of a solid fabric, as these prints add interest, yet act as a solid. Use 100% cotton fabric for appliqué, as it will hold a crease, making the edge easier to turn under.

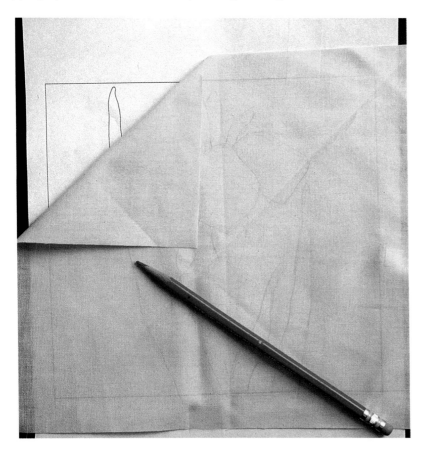

Cut the block 13" (31.2cm) or larger to add a little fabric insurance. The stitching of the appliqué may pucker the background fabric, making the square smaller. The block will be trimmed to 12½" (30cm) when you are finished with the appliqué. The sewn, finished size of the block in your quilt will be 12" (28cm).

Lightly mark or trace placement guidelines for the appliqué pieces onto the background fabric. Draw the full-size appliqué pattern on a sheet of paper or trace directly from the book, depending on the pattern. Place the pattern behind the background fabric and trace placement lines on the background fabric, using a light colored pencil, or any that will show on the fabric. These placement lines are used to position the parts of the appliqué on the background fabric. If you cannot see through the fabric, use a light table or cut the templates and trace the entire shape onto the top of the background fabric.

Single Layer Appliqué

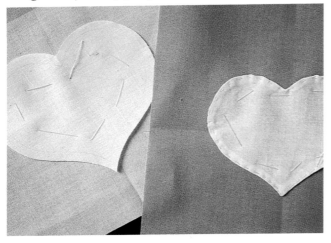

Materials Needed:
6" Background Fabric: Cut 2
6" Square Appliqué Fabric: Cut 2
Template Materials
Thread, Needles, Scissors, Pencil, Marking Pen

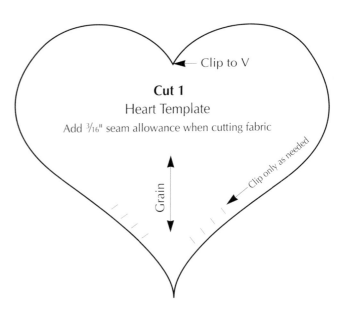

Clip to V

Cut 1
Heart Template
Add ³/₁₆" seam allowance when cutting fabric

Grain

Clip only as needed

The easiest appliqué to learn is the single layer appliqué. One large, curvilinear form is cut and basted to a background, using the pinch and needleturn method or the basted edge method. Hawaiian appliqué is a good example of single layer appliqué.

Use the heart pattern to practice. Read the basted edge and needleturn sections on the following pages. Practice one heart with each method of appliqué.

Trace the heart onto template material. Cut one heart out of the template plastic. Transfer the grainline onto the template. Label the template as indicated. Place the template right side up on the right side of the appliqué fabric. Match the grain line on the template to the grain line of the fabric.

Mark around the edge of the template with a pencil. This line is the turn-under line; mark lightly.

Cut two hearts, adding a scant ³/₁₆" (4.5mm) seam allowance, gauging the amount by eye.

When the appliqué is finished, decide whether you are going to hand quilt through the appliqué pieces. If so, trim the backing from behind the appliqué to reduce bulk and make that area easier to quilt.

Use small, sharp scissors to carefully cut the backing fabric away from the back of the appliqué. The extra thickness of the layers of the appliqué look nice and do not need to be trimmed away if you are not going to quilt in those areas.

Basted Edge Method

The basted edge method involves marking and cutting the shape, turning under the seam allowance along the marked line, and basting along the folded edge before the piece is basted onto the background. The basted edge method is best used when working with small pieces, a lot of pieces, when one piece covers another, and when great accuracy is needed. Although it takes more time than the needleturn method, the basted edge method yields very fine work.

Mark the guidelines on the 13" (31.2cm) background fabric to indicate where to place the appliqué pieces. Place the template on the right side of the appliqué fabric and mark around the edges.

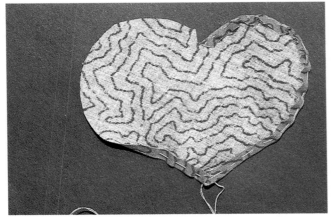

Cut out the pieces, adding a scant ³/₁₆" (4.5mm) seam allowance. Fold the seam allowance to the back. Using a short running stitch, sew ¹/₁₆" (1.5mm) in from the folded edge of the appliqué pieces. This stitching or basting along the folded edge will hold the seam allowance to the back.

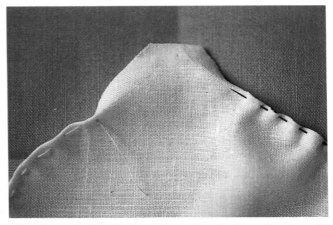

The closer the basting is to the edge, the less clipping will be necessary.

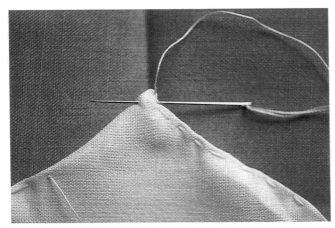

To appliqué the point of the heart, fold one side to the back, then fold the other side to the back. Take one holding stitch straight across the back.

Finish basting around the edge.

Position the appliqué pieces onto the background fabric, aligning the edges to the marked guidelines. Place the pieces in a layered manner if needed. Baste the pieces to the background. Use a blind hem stitch and matching cotton thread and appliqué the pieces to the background, following the instructions on the next page. Remove all bastings and press the block. Re-mark the block to 12½" (30cm) and trim to size.

The Blind Hem Stitch

The blind hem stitch is fast, and an easy stitch for beginners. The idea is to sew a stitch that barely shows along the edge of the appliqué. It is used successfully for most methods of appliqué.

Thread a size 9 Sharp or Between with a fairly short (12" to 15" [28-36cm]) single strand of cotton thread that closely matches the appliqué fabric. Tie a single knot on the longer end of the thread.

Wear a thimble on the longest finger of the hand holding the needle. The appliqué piece has been basted to the background fabric, approximately ¾" (1.8cm) in from the edge. The left hand helps to hold the appliqué to the background fabric. The right hand holds and pushes the needle to form the stitch.

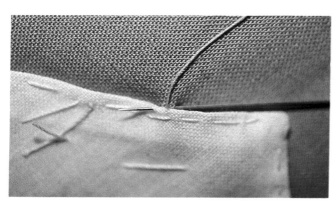

Bring the needle from the back to the front. Place the tip of the needle into the background fabric, slightly (¹⁄₆₄"—two threads' distance) behind where the thread came out of the appliqué's folded edge. Sew forward, pushing the needle and coming up through the front, barely catching the appliqué's edge (¹⁄₃₂" to ¹⁄₆₄"). Pull the needle and thread through. Tug the thread slightly. This slight pull on the thread tightens the stitch and locks it in place.

Continue this blind hem stitch around the appliqué. Sew the stitches close together (¹⁄₃₂"), or as comfortable.

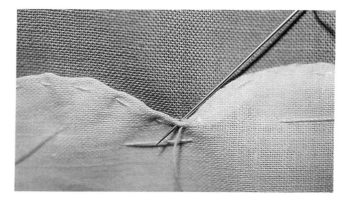

On inside curves and V's the stitches should be so close as to almost touch. On an inside curve or a sharp V cut into the seam allowance to within one thread from the fold-under line. Excess clipping weakens a seam—clip curves only as needed.

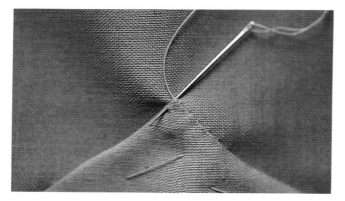

Sew an extra holding stitch at the tip of the points. Try to form smooth curves. If the fabric forms peaks where notches are cut, round out the seam line by placing the tip of the needle in the side seam fold and push the tip along the fold. This will help to form a smooth line.

The straighter the stitch on the back, the less the stitch will show on the front. When you have completed the appliqué or are almost out of thread (about 6" [15cm] left), push the needle straight through to the back. Form a small back stitch or two on the back, behind the edge of the appliqué. Trim the thread end. Remove the bastings and press.

The Pinch and Needleturn Method

The appliqué piece is basted to the background and the edges are turned under as you sew. The needleturn method is used when working with narrow points, curves, larger pieces, single layer, Broderie Perse, and Hawaiian quilting. The pinch and needleturn method may also be use for a layered design.

Once mastered, this method may be used for most appliqué.

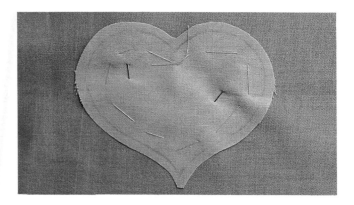

Position the appliqué pieces to match the marked guidelines on the background fabric.

Baste the appliqué to the background fabric, ¾" (1.8cm) in from the edge. Do not turn the edges under while basting.

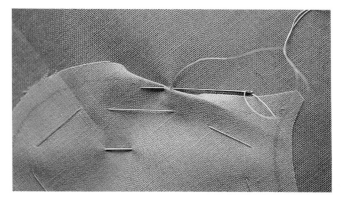

Hold the background fabric and appliqué piece with the thumb and forefinger of the left hand (if you're right-handed). Begin stitching in the straightest area.

Pinch and fold under the seam allowance ½" (1.2cm) ahead of the stitching. Start the first stitch from the back of the fabric, bringing the needle to the front into the fold of the appliqué. Pull the thread through to the top of the appliqué. Sew using the blind hem stitch. Take one stitch at a time. Pinch and turn the edge under ½" (1.2cm) ahead of the stitching.

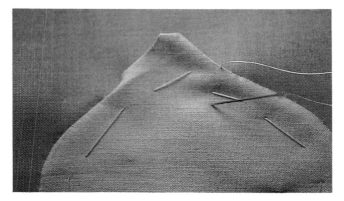

Use the tip of the needle to push under the fabric on very tight inside curves and to form points. On points, 1" or so before the point turn the tip back on one side, and then the other.

Stitches on inside curves should be very close together.

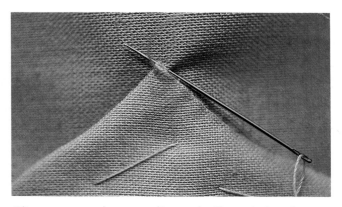

Clip seams to the seam line only if needed to form a smooth curve. Excess clipping will cause the edge to fray and make a weakened seam.

Trim excess seam allowances before they are turned under. Trim points as you sew to them.

Remove the basting stitches and press. Trim away the backing if desired.

Re-mark the block to 12½" (30cm) and trim to size.

See washing instructions, page 84.

Finishing the Top

Cutting Ideas

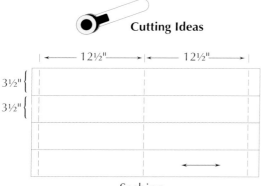

Sashing

Setting Squares

Sashing Strips and Setting Squares

The pieced and appliquéd Sampler blocks are placed in a balanced arrangement with or without sashing strips sewn between the blocks. Sashing strips are used to frame and separate the blocks, to enlarge the top and to provide an area to quilt. Large pieces of one fabric are usually used in the sashing. Thus, whatever color is used in the sash will add a lot of that color to the top. For example, if you want the top to appear more blue, use a blue sash. Quilting shows more on solid and tone-on-tone prints; use these fabrics in the sashing to showcase the quilting. A narrow sashing brings the blocks together. A wide sash separates each block and provides even more area to display the quilting. It is also an efficient way to make the quilt larger.

The "setting squares" are small squares of fabric used to divide the sashing strips and add some color to the sashing. Their seams are used as guide marks to pin to the blocks' seams and set the top together. This alignment helps to make the top straight, flat and square. Use a color in the squares to add a sparkle or highlight to the top, or feature one of your favorite fabrics used in the blocks, as these pieces will "walk" the eye across and unify the top.

Yardage estimates and quilt plans are given for 3" (7.5cm) wide finished sashing and 3" (7.5cm) square setting squares. The 3" x 12" (7.5 x 28cm) sashing strip and 3" (7.5cm) setting squares are chosen as a proportionate width for 12" (28cm) blocks, but any width may be used.

Use scissors, or the rotary cutter, mat, and cutting guide to cut the sashing and setting squares. Measure and mark the wrong side of the fabric. Fabric stretches more across the grain than lengthwise. Cut the long edge of the sashing on the lengthwise grain. This will stabilize the blocks. If the finished size of the sashing is to be 3" wide x 12" long (7.5 x 28cm), cut the strips 3½" x 12½" (8.4 x 30cm). Cut the setting squares 3½" x 3½" (8.4 x 8.4cm) if a 3" (7.5cm) sash is used. Refer to the quilt plans, and cut the amount needed to complete the top.

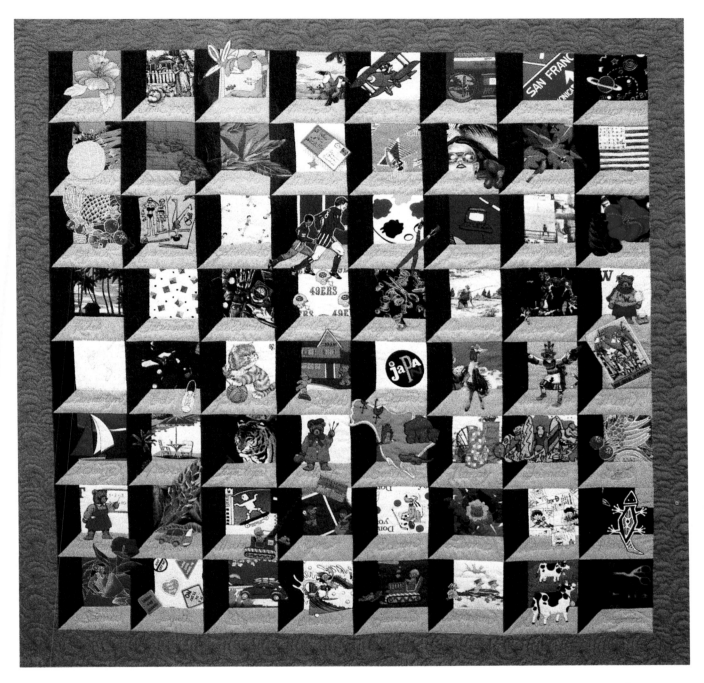

"My Favorite Things" Attic Window Quilt by Diana Leone, 1989. Hand and machine quilted. See Attic Window pattern page 92. The patchwork-appliqué technique was used to showcase the variety of fabrics. The names of the people and places associated with the fabrics were free machine quilted below each window.

Sewing the Sashing Strips to the Blocks

Some of the pieced blocks may be a little larger or smaller than the 12" (28cm) finished size needed. The top will be flat and square if you use match marks in the sashing to align to the seams in the blocks. To square and set the blocks to the sash, mark each sashing to correspond with the divisions of the block that will be sewn to it. Decide if there will be an outer row of sashing between the blocks and the border.

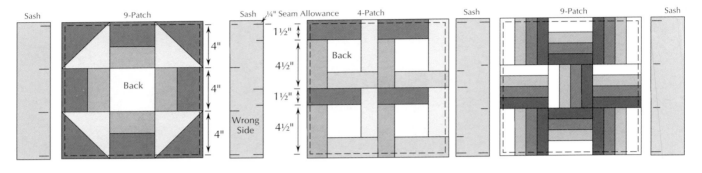

First mark ¼" (0.6cm) at each end of the sashing strips for the seam allowance. If one block is a 9-patch, mark the 12½" (30cm) sash at 4" (9.6cm) intervals. If the block is a 4-patch, mark the 12½" (30cm) sash into two equal sections of 6" (15cm).

Sew the vertical sash to the blocks. Mark the match marks on the sashing. Mark in the seam allowance, on the wrong side of the sashing. Pin the sashes to their corresponding blocks, easing as necessary to fit. Sew all of the vertical sashings to the blocks.

Sewing the Setting Squares to the Horizontal Sash

Sew the setting squares to the horizontal sashes. Mark match marks in the sashing to align to the seam lines. Pin and sew the rows together. Press the block seams toward sashing.

Trim all of the seams to a scant ¼" (0.6cm). Clip all loose threads.

Hawaiian Sampler Quilt designed by Diana Leone, pieced and quilted by Doris Olds.

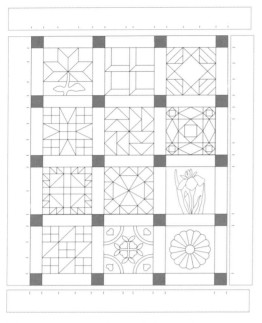

Match the seam lines of the lattice to the match marks along the border.

Borders

Borders are added to frame the blocks, to make the top the size needed, and to provide an area to showcase the quilting. The border may be made from one or more fabrics. The corners of the border may be mitered or squared. You may choose to miter all of the corners, or only the two corners at the foot of the bed. Directions for mitering are on the next page. The bottom corners may be rounded if the edges of the quilt reach the floor. Usually the side and bottom borders are the same width. The top border may be adjusted to center the pieced top on the bed.

Diagrams and yardage estimates are provided in the quilt plans on page 14. Measure the inner top across the middle vertically and horizontally and note the dimensions on your quilt plans. To determine exactly how wide to make the border, place the finished, borderless top on a bed, and measure the drop from the edge of the top down to the point where the quilt will fall on the side of the bed.

If you set aside long lengths of fabric for the borders earlier, use them now to cut the four border strips. Add ¼" (0.6cm) on each side and at the ends of the borders for the seam allowance. To allow for mitered corners, add a length at both ends that equals the width of the borders, plus an inch or two extra. Follow the diagram for square corners.

Mark the inside edge of the seam allowance of the border strips and every 3", 12", 3", (7.5, 28, 7.5cm), etc., as necessary to match the seams of the blocks and lattice. Pin the seams to match each mark, easing the blocks to fit the match marks. Sew the borders to the quilt top, starting with the sides, then the top and bottom. Miter the corners if desired. Press the seams toward the borders. Trim all of the seams and loose threads.

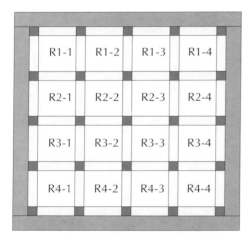

Top arranged with lattice, setting squares, and lattice around the outer edge.

Top arranged block-to-block, with no lattice.

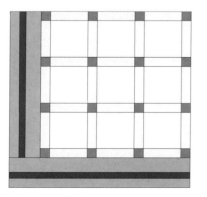

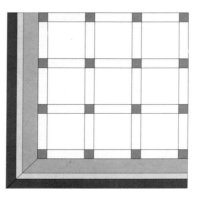

Border variations.

45° Mitered Corners

The mitered corner is used as a final finishing touch to showcase the top. The 45° angled seams look especially nice if the border is pieced, and when solid or tone-on-tone prints are used. Mitered corners are easy, and once you are successful you will want to use them on every top.

Sew the borders to the top allowing enough fabric to form the miters. (The additional lengths at each corner must be equal to the width of the borders, plus an inch or two extra). The seams holding the borders to the top must stop ¼" (0.6cm) from the outside edges—no more, no less.

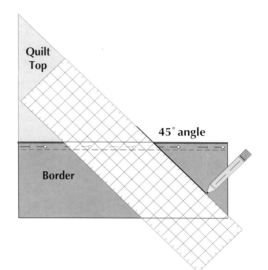

Fold the top on the diagonal, right sides together, forming a 45° angle. This fold is the guide for aligning the 45° marked template or cutting guide and for marking the angle on the border fabric. Place the folded top on the table in front of you, with two of the borders toward you. Align the border fabrics, right sides together, with their outer edges perfectly straight and even with each other. All of the border seam lines should be exactly on top of each other. Pin the two borders together, out of the way of the sewing line. Push the seam allowances toward the inner top fabric (away from the border) and pin in the seam allowances.

Place a triangular template or cutting guide with the 45° on top of the fold of the top, extending across the border at a 45° angle, and mark this angle very carefully, extending the fold line of the quilt across the border fabrics. Pin along the marked line.

Carefully lift the top, and place the marked, mitered seam line under the presser foot. Lower the needle into the border fabric *exactly* where the miter will begin. The seam allowances should be pushed back and away from the sewing line. Do not backstitch. Do not sew over the seam allowances. Sew from the inside corner, where the border and top fabrics meet, to the outside edge of the miter, following the marked line. Trim the mitered seams to ¼" (0.6cm), and trim the loose threads.

Repeat for the remaining corners. Press all of the seams away from the top. Press the mitered seams open, or to one side. Once you have mastered the mitered corner you'll be ready to make an Attic Window quilt!

Making a Rounded Corner

If any of the corners of the quilt are to be rounded, plan it now, before going on to marking and basting your quilt. Place the quilt top on the bed and position the corner the way it will drape. Place a safety pin at the top corner edge of the quilt. Measure from the safety pin to the floor, or where the edge of the quilt will be. Mark this point on the tape measure.

Place the quilt on a flat surface. Cut a piece of string the length needed based on the measurements from the safety pin to the mark on the tape measure, adding a few extra inches. Tie the string around a piece of chalk. Tie one end of the string to the safety pin. Make the distance from the safety pin to the chalk the measured length. Draw an arc from the side to the bottom with the chalk, forming a curved corner. Quilt to the line. After the top is quilted, cut the corner off along the marked, chalked line.

Assembling the Quilt

Marking a Quilting Design

Before the quilt is set together you will need to decide how much quilting you want to do. How soon do you need the quilt finished? How will the quilt be used, and by whom? Is it an heirloom to be handed down through generations, or is the quilt meant to be used and enjoyed? Will the quilt be hand or machine quilted, or a combination of both?

I recommend that beginners quilt just enough to hold the layers together and finish the project as soon as possible. Minimum quilting should be no less than every 6" (15cm). There are no set rules, as each quilt and circumstance is different. Quilt as much as you want. The Sampler provides an opportunity for you to practice different techniques. I will take you through the basic steps of hand quilting. For more complete information on hand quilting, refer to the Bibliography.

When you have decided how much and where you plan to quilt, mark the top with a wax-based or other removable pencil. Mark the lines using a ruler, stencil, template, or tracing design. In addition to, or instead of, marked lines, ¼" (0.6cm) wide masking tape may be placed along a seam line or quilting line to be used as a guide for quilting. Quilting "in-the-ditch" or along a seam line may also be done without marking.

Mark the blocks, sash, and border wherever you think you want to quilt. If you decide to quilt less when you get there, the lines will wash out. Mark away from the thick seam allowances whenever possible, as it is difficult to quilt across bulky seams.

Design Ideas

Generally speaking, if the quilt's designs are curvilinear, as in appliqué, straight line quilting is used in the background to complement, enhance and bring out the curved lines of the appliqué. Appliquéd blocks are usually outlined ⅛" (0.3cm) away from the appliqué, into the background fabric. Sometimes appliqué appears to be padded. Usually it is not—it is the quilting around the edge of the appliqué that puffs up the design. Patchwork blocks are enhanced with outline, in-the-ditch, straight lines or curved lines.

Any design may be marked onto the fabrics. Ideas for a quilting design are endless. Look at your fabrics to see if they contain a design that can be adapted for quilting or that inspires you to trace or even draw something similar. If you want to copy the fabric design, photocopy a section of fabric and trace the design onto white paper with a black felt marker. Books contain many suitable designs specifically made to trace and use on your quilt (see Bibliography). Use any pre-cut stencil, of which there are thousands.

Observe photographs and actual quilts—you can get a lot of good ideas from other quilts.

Tracing a Design

Any line drawing, black on white paper, can be traced onto most fabrics. Coloring books are good resources. Buy them during different holiday seasons to accumulate a good variety. Trace the design onto white paper. Go over the line with a black Sharpie™ felt pen to darken the lines.

Place the paper behind the quilt top, and trace the design onto the quilt top with the pencil. You can usually see the lines through light to medium fabrics (white to medium blue) well enough to trace the design. A light box can be used to trace onto dark fabrics. (See Supplies and Materials for details.)

Refer to the Bibliography for books with quilt designs that are made for you to trace, photocopy, enlarge or reduce and trace over.

Stencils

There are hundreds of sizes of accurately manufactured stencils in beautiful designs. Stencils are made of semi-rigid plastic sheets. Slits are cut in the plastic and used to draw lines on the quilt top. The stencil is placed on the quilt top and the lines are marked with a wax-based pencil. Areas of the stencil called "bridges" are left uncut in the stencils. These bridges need to be marked freehand, after the stencil is removed. Stencils can be used over and over.

Quilting Templates

In the old days, quilters used any household item that could be marked around as a template for their quilting lines. A cup, saucer or cookie cutter were common choices. Today you can still use any item to make a template to trace around. Make a template to trace around by cutting any shape out of the template plastic.

TIP
If you mismark, do not erase or try to remove your marks. Instead, change to a different color pencil. The lines will wash away.

Bridge

Remove stencil and draw a bridge connecting the lines.

← Slit in stencil

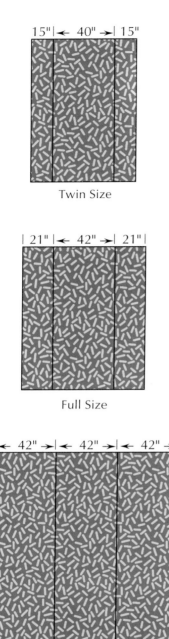

15" |← 40" →| 15"

Twin Size

| 21" |← 42" →| 21" |

Full Size

|← 42" →|← 42" →|← 42" →|

Queen or King Size

Preparing the Back

Use the same high quality 100% cotton fabric, either print or solid, that you used for the quilt top. Sheets are not recommended for quilt backs, as the threads are woven too closely, they are hard to quilt through, they don't wear the same as the yardage used for the front, and they may "pill." Use a print on the back of the quilt to hide the stitches, or if you are going to change thread colors often.

One 42" (105cm) width of fabric will back a wall or crib quilt up to 40" (96cm) wide. A quilt width of 40" to 82" (9.6 -19.6m) or wider will have to be pieced to make the fabric wide enough to cover the back. A quilt width larger than an 84" (20m) (queen/king) will need three lengths of fabric sewn together. Cut off the selvages before piecing the back. The back should be made at least 2" (5cm) larger than the top on all four sides.

To piece the back, use one center panel 42" (105cm) wide by the full length of the back, then split one 42" (105cm) length down the middle and sew the halves to the sides of the center panel. A full 42" (105cm) width in the center helps the quilt drape over the bed. A center seam will draw up, not look as good, and will not lie flat on the bed.

"Gwendolyn's Quilt" backart. The front of the quilt is shown on page 3.

Creatively Pieced Back

Most quilters purchase more fabric than they can use for the front of the quilt. Use the leftover fabrics, any new fabrics, and your imagination to creatively piece the back of your quilt. It is best to make the back simple, as the added bulk of the seams on the back will be more difficult to hand quilt.

Back art is in. The book *Backart—On the Flip Side* from Leone Publications provides inspiration and instruction.

Basting the Layers of the Quilt

Properly basting the quilt is a very important step toward successful finishing. If the quilt will be hand quilted, baste the quilt with thread. If the quilt will be machine quilted, you may safety-pin baste the layers together.

The top, batt and back are layered on a large, flat, waist-high surface. The basting stitches or pins hold the layers together so that the quilt can be quilted with or without a hoop or a frame. Basting stitches are made with a long Milliner's needle and strong white thread. The stitches are taken from the center out in horizontal and vertical rows every 3"- 5" (7.5-12cm). The closer the rows of basting, the more flat and smooth the quilt will be and the better prepared it will be for handling during the quilting process; over-basting is better than under-basting.

I discovered long ago that I could baste any size quilt on a large table. A ping-pong table is great, but a large dining room table is fine. A fold-out cardboard cutting board on top of a smaller table will work if your space is limited. Cover a good table with a plastic tarp or shower curtain to protect it from the needles. Do not baste on the floor, as it is too hard on your body. Put books or blocks of wood under the table legs to make a lower table waist-high. This makes the basting process easier on your back.

TIPS

A well-basted quilt enables you to quilt with or without a hoop, in your lap or in a frame.

To remove wrinkles in the batting, hold a hairdryer set to warm 6"-10" above the surface of the batting, or place the batting in a cool dryer.

Make big knots on the end of the doubled thread. It will be easy to pull on the knots to remove the basting threads when the quilting is finished.

Drunkard's Path quilt pieced by Corinne Lorentzen. Wall Sampler quilt pieced by Ann Gage, and machine quilted by Laura Lee Fritz.

Gravity will hold the layers together—no pinning is necessary. If the quilt top is smaller than the top of the table, a few strips of masking tape along the backing's edges will hold the back to the table. If the quilt is larger than the top of the table, portions of the quilt top, batting, and back will hang over the edges of the table.

Only the part of the quilt that is on the top of the table is basted. After the portion that is on the table is basted, the areas hanging over the edge are pulled to the top of the table and basted. It is much easier to baste a quilt if you have someone help you—ask a friend to help you baste.

Mark the center of the edge of both ends of the table. Mark the center of the top and bottom of the batting, quilt top, and backing fabric.

Place the backing fabric wrong side up on the table. Match the center of the back with the marked center of the table. Make certain that the back is smooth and wrinkle-free, as you will not be able to put your hands under the quilt to straighten the backing while you are basting.

Carefully center the batting over the back.

Place the quilt's top over the batting, right side up. Align the centers of the edges together. If you have someone to help, ask them to hold the backing at one end of the table. Gently pull the backing to make sure that it is flat and smooth. Do not run your hands over the top, as you will push wrinkles into the backing and you won't be able to see them.

Once the back is pulled smooth you can begin to baste.

TIPS

Tape or clamp the quilt back to the table. A taut, flat back is best.

To pin-baste for machine quilting, layer the quilt as in hand basting. Use brass or nickel coated rust-proof pins, size 1 or 0 as desired. Pin at least every 4-5" over the entire top.

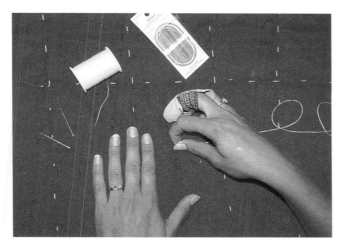

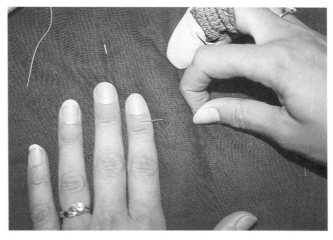

Thread six or eight Milliner's or long darner needles with doubled thread long enough to reach from the center of the quilt to the edge of the quilt. Knot the ends of the thread. Begin in the center and baste from the center out.

Hold the top of the quilt down with the left hand (if you're right-handed). Push the needle into the quilt with the right hand, going all the way through the layers and coming out through the top about 1" (2.4cm) away.

Basting stitches are fairly long. Take two or three stitches, then pull the full length of thread through the quilt; using a double thread makes it strong enough to pull the thread.

Forming a few stitches and then pulling the thread through saves time and keeps your arm from tiring.

Baste to the edge of the table, or to the edge of the quilt if it is a small quilt.

If the quilt is larger than the table, leave the threaded needle in the quilt when you reach the edge of the table. Do not backstitch until you have basted to the edge of the quilt.

With a new needle and thread, begin again in the center of the quilt, 3"- 5" (7.5-12cm) away from the last row.

Baste to the table's edge, once again leaving the threaded needle in the quilt at the edge of the table. Baste all of the quilt's surface from the center out to all edges of the table, leaving the threaded needles in the quilt all along the edges of the table.

When the center area is basted, gently pull the quilt so that an area that was hanging over the edge is now on the top of the table. Using the needles that you've already threaded, continue basting this area out to the edges of the table (if the quilt is still larger than the table) or to the edge of the quilt.

Backstitch at the edge of the quilt. Clip the thread. Baste until the entire top is basted horizontally and vertically every 3"-5" (7.5-12cm). Turn the quilt over to see if there are any pleats or wrinkles in the backing. If there are, take out the basting and re-baste.

Bring the extra backing around to the front over the batting, and hand baste along the edges of the quilt. This will keep the edges neat and the batting from wearing thin during the quilting process. When the quilting is completed and the quilt is ready to be bound, the excess batting and backing will be trimmed.

Quilting

After the quilt top has been marked, layered with the batt and backing, and basted, it is ready to be quilted by hand or machine. Quilting is the process of stitching through the top, batt and backing, by hand or machine in a design that enhances the overall beauty of the quilt. The primary function of quilting is to hold these layers together securely enough to last the lifetime of the quilt. A secondary and equally important function is to add a surface design and interest to the quilt.

The quilting is the reward of the piecemaker. The Sampler Quilt provides you with an opportunity to experiment with different quilting techniques. Try practicing with a variety of needles, threads, thread colors, thimbles, quilt designs, and hoops to find what tools you most enjoy using.

There is much to be said for the hand quilting process. First, it is important that you are taking precious time and using it to work on a personal project. Second, there is a calm quietness that involves you in the process. Finally, there is beauty in the finished project, appreciated by all who see it.

There are many more reasons why hand quilting is worthwhile, but if you do not have the time or inclination, you can successfully machine quilt any project. If you opt to machine quilt, be sure that you learn to do it properly. The quilt is large, bulky, and heavy. In the machine quilting process, half of the quilt must be rolled tight enough to fit inside the arm of the machine. It takes less time to machine quilt, but it is strenuous work when dealing with a double or larger quilt.

I wrote the book *Fine Hand Quilting*, published by Leone Publications, which covers every aspect of hand quilting and provides you with a thorough foundation in all of the processes involved in hand quilting.

Refer to the Bibliography for additional books on machine and hand quilting.

Supplies

Hoop: (*select one*) 14" to 24" round, oval, or
        Q-Snap™ frame 11" x 17" or 17" x 17",
        a hoop on a floor stand, or a quilt frame
Needles: Sizes 9, 10, or 12 Betweens
Thread: 100% cotton
Thimble: Leather or metal, one or two
Scissors: Small, blunt, sharp
¼" Drafting or masking tape
Bag balm
Beeswax
Pin cushion with emery-filled strawberry
Needle grabber or small balloon
Needle threader
Tape for underfinger
Good lighting—*if you are using a hoop, your light
   source should be over your left shoulder if you
   are right-handed; and over your right shoulder if
   you are left-handed; or in front, shining on the quilt*
A comfortable chair
The quilt

The Quilting Process

There are many techniques used to hand quilt. Each method has its advantages and restrictions. I again recommend that you try many techniques and choose what works best for you. You may use a hoop held in the lap, a hoop with a floor stand, a frame, or you may even quilt in your lap without a hoop. If you baste the quilt well, you will be able to quilt it using the method which is most comfortable for you.

Quilting in a hoop provides portability. It also allows you to turn the quilt, so that you can quilt in any direction. You will find that the most difficult part of quilting with a hoop is not being able to use the thumb of the holding hand. It is also necessary to prop the hoop on something stable, like the edge of a table in order to free the hands to quilt. Quilting without a hoop provides even more portability, but holding a larger portion of the quilt in one hand becomes tiring.

When selecting quilting thread, use colors that contrast, blend or closely match the quilt top—the choice is yours. I prefer thread colors that contrast slightly so that the quilting shows. It is okay to use different colors of thread on one quilt. I have used over twenty different colors in one quilt.

Place the center of the quilt over the bottom ring of the hoop. Place the top ring over the quilt. Tighten the ring. Some like it taut, some not. Try it fairly taut in the hoop at first. Wax the thread and thread the needle, put on the thimble, and sit comfortably with very good light. Quilt out from the center of the quilt. Quilt from right to left, or across the front of you. Turn the hoop as needed.

The goal in hand quilting is to form straight even stitches with the same amount of quilting thread showing on the top as the space between. A stitch is counted by how many are showing in one inch on the top. Five to six stitches per inch is great for beginners. Don't worry about length at first; straight stitches are more important in the beginning. Shorter stitches will come with practice. Concentrate on your stitches as you form them, and think about what each finger is doing in the process. Your stitches will improve with experience. Don't go back and take out your first stitches or you'll never finish your project.

When you quilt in a hoop or frame, you can't use the thumb of the holding hand. This is frustrating, and adds to the awkwardness. Take your time and practice. The forefinger or long finger of the underhand receives the prick of the sharp needle. I like to feel the tip of the needle on the pad of the finger. The needle is pushed back up into the quilt with the underfinger. You will develop a callous on that finger after a period of time. Use a band-aid or a piece of tape to protect the underfinger. Some people use a second metal thimble on the underfinger with great results. Michael James best describes this method in his book *The Quiltmaker's Handbook*. (See Bibliography).

I stated earlier that the quilting stitch is a running stitch. I didn't say that it was easy! As a beginner, you will find it very awkward to hold a short needle, use a thimble on a finger, hold a heavy, bulky quilt in a round hoop and not be able to use the thumb of the holding hand. But persevere—it will be worth the effort!

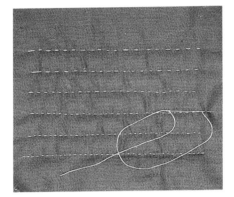

TIPS

Release the hoop's tension when you leave the quilt for a few hours. The tight hoop may leave a stretch ring in the quilt.

Leave the quilt out where you can see it. You'll be more likely to pick it up and work on it.

Threading the Needle

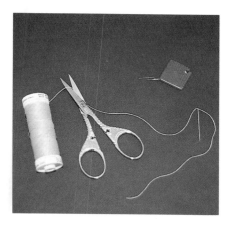

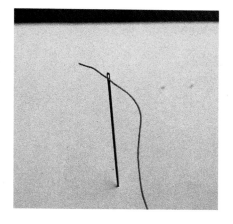

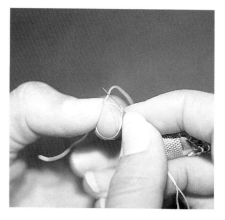

Thread the needle while the thread is still attached to the spool. Cut the loose end of the thread at a slight angle before threading the needle.

If you're not using a needle threader, steady your elbows on a table.

Hold the thread ½" (1.2cm) from the end in your right hand. Hold the needle's eye over a piece of white paper or something light so that you can see the hole. Hold the needle in your left hand. Push the thread into the needle's eye.

Pull about 18" (45cm) of thread off of the spool. This length is used so that the thread won't twist and wear out. Cut the thread at the spool.

Use a single strand of thread to quilt. Tie a single knot on the end that was cut from the spool.

Waxing the Thread

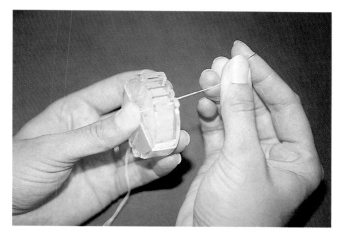

Most quality thread manufactured for hand quilting is treated with a coating to make the thread smooth. I still recommend waxing the thread, as I find that it sews more easily, keeps it from twisting, and helps to keep the thread clean. You cannot help getting the thread dirty with so much handling. The wax keeps the dirt on the surface of the thread, and this dirt will be easily removed when the quilt is washed.

The thread will fray at the needle's eye if you pinch the eye with the side of the thimble. Use the end of the thimble to push the needle. Move the needle along the thread as it is used. Re-wax the thread to mend the frayed area. The tail end will fray with use; trim it whenever you notice fraying.

Single Stitch

The quilting hand (the right hand if you are right-handed, or the left hand if you are left-handed) is on top of the quilt, holds the needle with the thumb and forefinger, and pushes with the thimble on the middle finger. The "underhand" is under the quilt; the forefinger or middle finger receives the tip of the needle and pushes it back up into the quilt. Both hands work together.

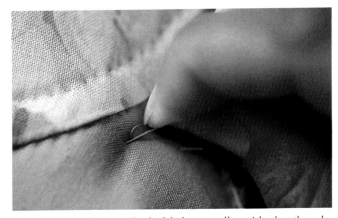

Place the tip of the threaded needle on top of the quilt, ½" (1.2cm) away from where you want to begin. Slip the needle between the layers, coming out through the top with the needle's tip where you want to begin quilting. Gently pull the thread through to "pop" the knot between the layers. This hides the knot between the layers.

If the knot pulls through too easily, make the knot a little larger. If it is difficult to pop, rub your fingernail over the knot.

To form the first stitch, hold the needle with the thumb and forefinger of your writing hand. Place the tip of the needle on the marked line ½" (1.2cm) ahead of where you want to begin to quilt. Draw the tip of the needle back to exactly where you want the needle to form the length of the first stitch and where the tip of the needle will go into the quilt.

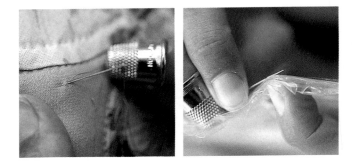

Barely insert the tip of the needle into the quilt. Hold the eye of the needle firmly by the indents in the end or side of the thimble. The end of your forefinger or the middle finger of your underhand will feel the tip of the needle. The tip of the needle should barely touch your underfinger.

The underfinger curls forward when it is touched by the tip of the needle, and the nail or end of the finger firmly pushes the tip of the needle back up into the back of the quilt, forming the stitch on the back.

Release the thumb and forefinger that were pushing or holding the needle into the quilt, and pull the tip of the needle all the way through the quilt. You have now formed one stitch.

Repeat this procedure forming one stitch at a time. Slightly pull on the thread. The thread should slightly sink into the fabric, but not so much as to gather the stitching.

Practice one stitch at a time until you are comfortable with the new tools.

Multiple Stitches

A fast, efficient, and accurate method of quilting is to form two or more stitches on a Between needle before pulling it through. I refer to these multiple stitches as "rock 'n roll" stitches. The number of stitches that you will be able to form will depend on the length of the stitches, the length of the needle, the thickness of the quilt, and whether you are quilting a straight or curved line. Four to five stitches will usually fill the needle of a ½" (1.2cm) thick quilt. You may only be able to form one or two stitches at a time on curved lines, depending on the obliqueness of the curve. On straight lines, form as many stitches as you can on the needle, leaving enough room on the needle to grip it and pull it through the layers.

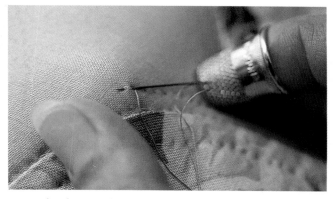

Form the first stitch as you did for a single stitch, but do not push the needle completely through the top. Place the thimble at the end of the needle. The thimble is now controlling the needle. The end of the thimble pulls the end of the needle up and perpendicular to the surface of the quilt. Use an indent in the side or end of the thimble to barely push the needle into the quilt.

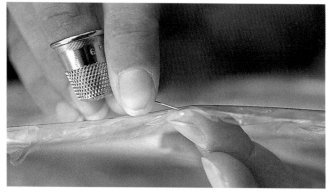

Insert the needle until the tip is barely touching your underfinger. When approximately ¹⁄₁₆" (1.5mm) of the needle is pushed through to the back, the underfinger will feel the tip. Use the underfinger to firmly push the tip back up and into the back of the quilt. Push the tip of the needle through to the top, so that only as much of the tip of the needle shows that is equal to the length of the stitch you want to form.

Repeat this "rock 'n roll" until the needle is full.

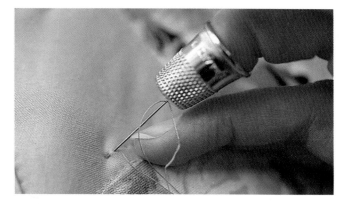

When you see the tip of the needle coming through the surface, use the indent in the side or end of the thimble to hold and pull the eye end of the needle straight up in an arc and push the tip down into and through the quilt again. The thumb of the upper hand gently pushes the quilt down in front of the tip of the needle.

Repeat these steps until the needle is filled with as many stitches as will fit on the needle (approximately 4-5), while still allowing enough room to grasp the tip.

Push the needle through to the top with the thimble, grasp the tip of the needle with a small balloon or rubber needle grabber, and pull the needle through the quilt.

Pull the thread just enough so that the stitches sink into the surface, but not enough to gather or pucker the quilt. The stitches on the back of the quilt may appear to be too short or crooked. This is caused by the needle entering the top parallel to the surface of the quilt or at an angle. If the needle is inserted more perpendicular to the surface, the stitches on the back will be longer and more even.

Ending the Thread

When you have at least 6" (15cm) of thread left, stop quilting and form a single knot at the surface before finishing the last stitch. Hold the thread straight up from the top of the quilt with the left hand.

With your right hand, hold the needle and go clockwise around the thread, coming around the held thread and forming a loop.

Pull the loop down to the surface of the quilt by placing the forefinger of the left hand over the loop.

A knot will form close to the surface, leaving just enough room ($\frac{1}{16}$" [1.5mm]) to finish the last stitch.

A second technique used to force the knot to form at the surface is to place the tip of the needle into the quilt, through the loop next to where the thread came out of the top. Pull on the thread and the knot will form on the surface.

Slip the needle between the layers. Exit ½" (1.2cm) away and tug on the thread, popping the knot between the layers. I do not backstitch. Pull on the thread tail and trim it with blunt pocket scissors.

Two Thimble Technique

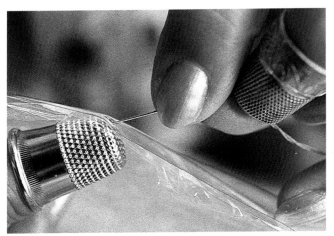

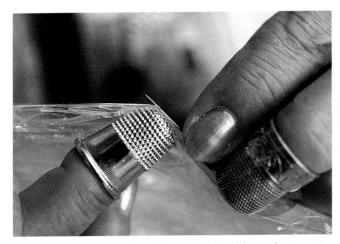

This technique is a very good method to learn, as you can quilt very fast, form very small stitches, and the underfinger does not get sore. The needle touches the bottom edge of the thimble on the underhand. The bottom thimble pushes the needle back up into the quilt.

Michael James introduced the two thimble technique in 1975. Practice this method and you will quickly become an expert.

Quilting in the Seam Line

Quilting in the seam line is referred to as "quilting in the ditch." Quilting exactly into the seam will hold the seam down, and is adequate to quilt a Sampler Quilt. Quilting in the seam line is fast, and it is a good technique for a beginner to use to practice quilting, as the stitching doesn't show very much.

Outline Quilting

Quilting ¼" (0.6cm) away from the seams is called outline quilting or "echo quilting." Outline quilting is done next to patchwork seams and into the background, echoing the edges of appliqué.

Echo quilting is the traditional technique used in Hawaiian quilting.

Quilting through Seams—the Poke & Stab Stitch

As much as possible, avoid quilting where the seam allowances are inside the quilt. There will be times, though, when you will want to quilt through the seams. When you want to quilt through the bulky seam areas, use the "poke and stab" stitch.

To quilt these areas, form single stitches by pushing the needle straight down through the layers. Pull the needle all the way through the back. Insert the needle into the back and return it to the front. Pull on the needle with a needle grabber or a small balloon. It is hard to turn the quilt over to see where to insert the needle.

Be careful that the part of the stitch showing on the back stays as straight as possible.

To "see" where to insert the needle into the back, place the tip of the needle 1" (2.4cm) ahead of where you want it to go into the back. Draw the tip back firmly against the back. You will see the top of the quilt rise up as the needle is being pulled against the back. You will be able to "feel" or see where you want the tip of the needle to go into the back of the quilt. Push the needle up, pull it through and continue on.

Masking Tape as a Quilting Guide

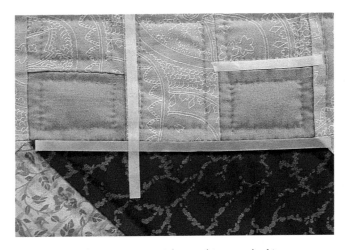

Use a strip of ¼" (0.6cm) wide masking or drafting tape as a removable guide for straight outline quilting. Tape may be placed next to a seam or anywhere else on the quilt and used as a guide. Tape can be used as a guide anytime—for example, when the pencil lines won't show on the printed fabric, or as an easy guide when quilting on dark fabrics.

Place one edge of the tape along the seam line. Quilt along the other edge of the tape. As you reach the end of the tape, move the tape and continue. Do not leave the tape on the quilt overnight as it may leave some of the glue on the fabric. A ¼" (0.6cm) flexible tape is available that can be used to outline next to curved seams.

Meander Quilting

Free-form hand guided quilting is especially useful in machine quilting.

Quilting the Sashing Strips, Border and Backing

Quilting stitches show more on solids than on textured or contrast prints. To showcase the quilting, use solids or tone-on-tone background prints for the sashing and border.

Edges

Quilt to the edges, with or without a hoop. If you use a round hoop, sew a length of fabric to the quilt's edge so it will fill the hoop and help to keep the quilt taut. I like to use the rectangular Q-Snap™ hoop along the edges.

Removing the Basting Stitches

To remove all basting stitches, carefully clip any backstitches. Pull on the knots, and remove the complete lengths of the basting threads. I use blunt pocket scissors to trim any tails of the quilting threads at this time. Trim the edges of the quilt so that they are even and as square as possible. Use an L-square on the corners and a straight edge along the edges. Machine stitch ⅛"- ¼" (0.3-0.6cm) in from the edges.

Tips

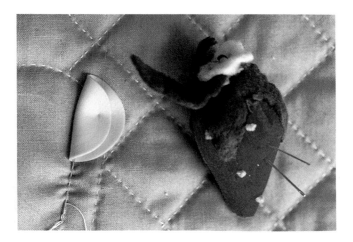

Refocus your eyes occasionally to avoid eyestrain. Listen to TV and look up. Listen to books on tape. Watch the leaves fall or the flowers grow, but do refocus as eye strain can make you ill.

I always leave my work with a threaded needle. It's part of my full-cup philosophy: I'm ready to pick up my work at any time and continue on.

Thread many needles in the morning. You will look forward to quilting, or any sewing, if the needles are ready.

If the edge of the metal thimble rubs the eye of the needle, the thread will break. Use the end of the thimble to push the needle.

Hold the needle in line with the quilting direction when entering the stitching line. This will help to keep the stitches straight.

Try not to angle the needle when entering the quilt. Twisted thread and angled stitches will result.

Clip the bastings as you quilt to them. Do not split a basting thread with a quilting stitch.

Quilt with many threaded needles in any direction. Leave the needles at the edge of the hoop. Move the hoop and continue on with the threaded needle.

If some batting comes through with the thread, you are using too much wax or the batt isn't bonded.

Crooked stitches show more on straight lines. Curves hide crooked stitches.

To eliminate twisted thread, stop every few stitches and roll the needle in the opposite direction of the twist.

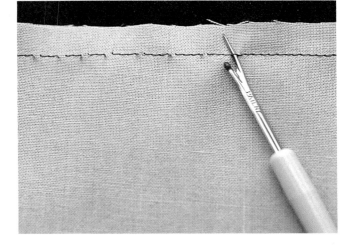

To easily remove unwanted seams, push the dull tip of the seam ripper under every third stitch one one side of the seam, and push upward, cutting the stitch. Pull on the thread on the other side to remove the thread.

Binding the Quilt

YARDAGE YIELD ▼ CHART				
Bias Cut Width	¾ yd. equals 27" sq.	1 yd. equals 36" sq.	1¼ yd. equals 45" sq.	1¾ yd. equals 60" sq.
1"	23 yd.	31 yd.	40 yd.	54 yd.
1½"	15 yd.	21 yd.	26 yd.	35 yd.
2"	12 yd.	16 yd.	20 yd.	27 yd.
➤ 2½"	9 yd.	12 yd.	16 yd.	21 yd.
2¾"	8 yd.	11 yd.	15 yd.	19 yd.
3"	7 yd.	10 yd.	13 yd.	18 yd.

A square is used to make continuous bias. Choose the size needed from the chart above.

- 27" square (¾ yd x ¾ yd)
- 36" square (1 yd x 1 yd)
- 45" square (1¼ yd x 1¼ yd)
- 60" square (1¾ yd x 1¾ yd)

Trim off selvages before using.

Binding quilts is a reward for finishing the project. I use double-fold bias binding made from one of the same quality fabrics in the quilt. Double-fold bias binding wears well and gives the edge the look, feel and weight that matches the quilted project. Bias binding is also best for curves, as it will ease and stretch around the curves as needed to fit.

The fabric used for the binding should be of the same quality as the fabric you use for the quilt top. The bias is cut as a continuous strip. 2½"-wide bias when folded and applied creates a double ½" binding on the front and back, which is an appropriate width for most quilts. The bias strip is folded in half, wrong sides together, and pressed. The raw edges of the bias are sewn to the front edge of the quilt by machine, using a walking foot. The folded edge of the bias is brought to the back of the quilt and sewn by hand, using matching thread and the blind hem stitch.

A Bias Yardage Yield Chart for the most commonly used widths of bias is included at the left. Select the square that will yield the lineal yardage needed to bind your project.

1. Cut the Square on the Diagonal

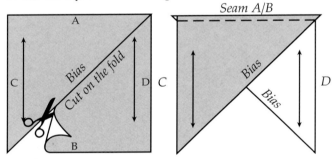

Mark A, B, C, and D in the seam allowance, on the wrong side of the fabric. Fold the fabric on the diagonal.

Cut on the diagonal. Place A and B right sides together, overlapping the seam ends of A and B ½".

Sew A and B together using a ½" seam allowance.

Press the seam open.

2. Measure and Mark the Cut Width

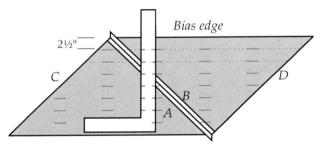

Determine how wide to make the bias. Place an L-Square or a yardstick on the wrong side of the fabric and mark the desired finished-cut width of the bias.

Move the L-Square and mark again. Connect the marks with a straight line.

3. Making the Tube

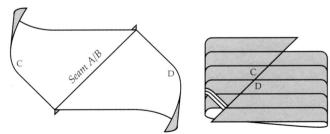

Turn right side up. Bring C and D together, right sides together.

Drop seam C/D down one bias width at the top and the bottom. Match the marked lines.

Pin the C/D seam, right sides together where the marked lines cross. Sew C and D together using a ½" seam allowance. Sew through the x's.

4. Cutting the Continuous Bias

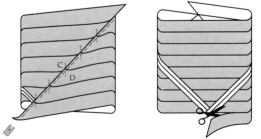

Press the seam open. Cut the continuous bias on the marked lines.

Fold bias rightside out and press gently.

5. Applying the Binding

Trim all of the edges of the quilt sandwich even and square, using a large (6" x 24") cutting guide, mat and rotary cutter.

Use a walking foot on the machine. Stay stitch (6 to 8 stitches per inch) ¼" in from the edge around the perimeter of the quilt.

Pin the edge of the double-folded, pressed binding to a bottom side edge of the project. Pin just 3 or 4 pins to hold the binding in place. (There is no need to pin the binding all the way around, as the binding may need to be eased while sewing.)

6. Sewing the Binding to the Quilt

Use the walking foot to sew the binding to the project. Begin sewing 4" down from the top of the folded end of the bias, toward the first corner. Sew a seam allowance slightly less than the width of the finished bias (e.g. ⅜" for a ½" bias). The quilt should fill the binding. Do not stretch the binding during the application.

Stop sewing exactly ½" from the corner. Turn the hand wheel and lift the needle out of the fabric.

7. Forming the Miter on the Front

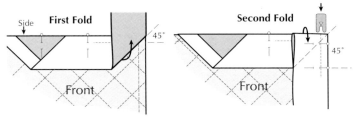

To make the first fold, turn the project one quarter turn counterclockwise. Fold the binding up at a 45° angle.

To make the second fold, fold the binding back down on top of itself, with the top fold of the bias flush with the top edge of the quilt. Align the edges of the bias with the edge of the project. Lower the walking foot. Sew from the top edge down to the next corner.

Repeat and miter all of the corners.

8. Ending the Binding

Place the unsewn end over the folded end. Cut enough bias to tuck it into the folded end (½" to 1"). Cut the unfinished end at a 45° angle.

Tuck the cut end into the folded end. Sew across the edges of the binding.

Trim any uneven edges of the quilt's layers to ⅜".

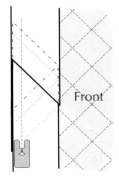

9. Forming the Miter on the Front and Back

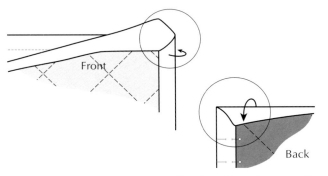

Fold the side of the bias to the back. Pull and square the corner.

Fold the top to the back, forming the mitered corner on the back. Pin the fold edge to the back. The folded edge on the back should cover the machine stitches.

10. Hemming the Binding

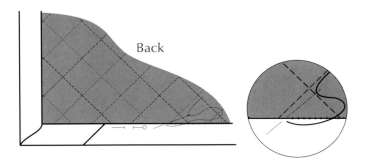

Sew along the fold edge using a blind hem stitch and a single knotted thread. Sew the corners to the point and back to the fold edge.

Lightly press the binding when finished.

Signing the Quilt

It is important to sign and date your quilt. If you are the maker of the top as well as the quilter, quilt your name into the quilt. If you make the top only, embroider your name on the front of the quilt. The information can go anywhere you like on the quilt.

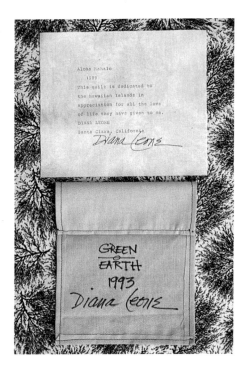

Another way of identifying your quilt is to take a piece of muslin, put it in a typewriter, and type the information onto the fabric, or just write your name on a piece of fabric with a fine tip permanent marker.

Sew the fabric label onto a lower corner of the back of your quilt. There are many ways of signing your name onto your quilt, some of them very elaborate. Refer to the Bibliography for books on signing.

Cleaning the Quilt

I recommend hand or machine washing quilts used on beds once a year or as needed. A quilt can be washed gently in the washing machine, if it is very stable. A quilt hanging on a wall may be gently vacuumed occasionally to keep it clean. Use the brush attachment and hold it slightly away from the surface while vacuuming.

Dry cleaning is not recommended for a quilt made of 100% cotton fabrics. If you want the cleaners to wash the quilt, you have to ask them. Some cleaners have an air drying rack where they can lay the quilt flat and circulate air to dry it. This may be expensive, but it is ideal.

Machine Washing

If the quilt was made within the last ten years, and it is very stable, it can safely be machine washed and dried. Resew any open seams and replace any torn patches before washing.

Before washing, be sure to test any washing liquid by placing a diluted drop of it on the fabric. If the color changes or blots off onto a clean towel, try a milder soap. Ivory Liquid, Easy Wash, Orvus (quilt soap), or any soap that does not contain phosphorous is fairly safe.

Wash the quilt on a gentle cycle. Set the dryer to cool. Place the quilt in the dryer with a large, dry towel. The towel acts as a buffer and helps absorb moisture. The quilt will dry very quickly with a towel.

Check the quilt every ten minutes. Take the quilt out of the dryer before it is completely dry. Place towels on the floor. Shake out the quilt, place it on top of the towels, and finish drying it at room temperature. If you have a clothesline, use it to air the quilt.

Hand Washing

The finished blocks, especially the appliqué, may need to be washed due to the handling. Use a mild soap and gently hand wash the block. Dry on a flat surface. Place the block face down on a terry towel and press gently. Turn the block right side up. Place a press cloth over the top and press gently. Use steam as needed.

To treat your quilt with care, as with any old quilt or a newly made heirloom, hand wash the quilt. Hand washing a quilt is hard work. It might take two days to soak, rinse, and air dry a large quilt. It is best to dry the quilt on a slightly overcast fall or spring morning.

Fill a bathtub with lukewarm water. Add one cup of mild soap such as Orvus or Easy Wash. Do not use soap that is recommended for wool, as it may yellow or bleach the fabrics. Place the quilt in the bathtub and push it up and down gently for a few minutes. Continue pushing it up and down in the water every 20 minutes. Let it soak for an hour or so. Drain the water.

Fill the tub with lukewarm water again and agitate the quilt by hand. Re-soap if necessary. Drain the tub, fill it again, agitate and rinse until the water runs clear. Squeeze out as much water as possible.

Place a large piece of plastic on a flat surface in the yard. Place a dry sheet over the plastic.

Place the wet quilt on a large towel and take it outdoors. Place the wet quilt on the sheet. Turn the quilt over every hour or so. If there is a lot of sun, place a clean sheet over the quilt while it is drying. Dry the quilt in the shade if at all possible. If you have a clothesline, hang the quilt between two lines.

Place the almost-dry quilt in a large dryer. Place a large dry towel in the dryer. Finish drying for 10-15 minutes.

Hanging the Quilt

The easiest way to hang a quilt is to sew a sleeve along the top edge of the back of the quilt, put a 2" (5cm) wide board through the sleeve, and tack the ends of the board to the wall. A ½ (43cm) yard of fabric yields an 84" (20m) length of two 9" (21.6cm) wide strips of fabric sewn together; ¾ yard (27" [64.8cm]) of fabric yields 129" of 9" (30m x 21.6cm) wide fabric.

Cut 9" (21.6cm) wide strips of fabric and piece them together to measure the exact width of the quilt from edge to edge. Fold ½" (1.2cm) in at each end, and stitch down by machine.

Fold the width of the strip in half, right-sides together, and sew ½" (1.2cm) from the raw edges by machine. Turn the tube inside out and press, or fold the raw edges to the back.

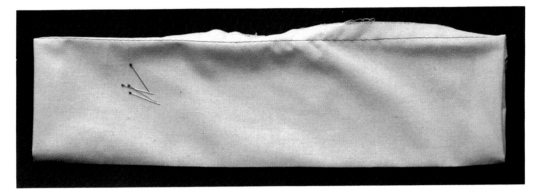

Pin the seam edge to the top of the quilt, aligning the edge of the sleeve to the seam line of the binding.

Sew the top edge of the sleeve to the quilt by hand, using a blind hem stitch. Sew the bottom of the sleeve to the quilt by hand.

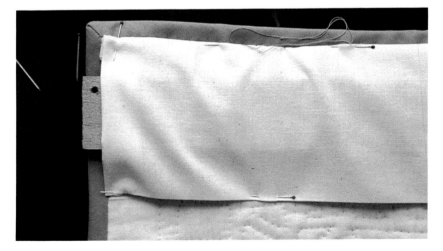

Buy a strip of plain moulding, ½" x 2" (1.2cm x 5cm) x the exact width of the quilt, less ½" (1.2cm). Place the board through the sleeve.

Put a finishing nail ¼" (0.6cm) in from each end of the board. Nail the board to the wall, or drill a hole ¼" (0.6cm) in from each edge of the board and hang the board with fish line from eye screws placed in the ceiling. The edges of the quilt should cover the ends of the wood.

Storing the Quilt

The quilt can be stored safely for a long period of time. One way is to roll the quilt on a long tube wrapped in acid-free tissue paper or in a clean sheet. It can then be stored under a bed or in a dark closet. I saw a closet in an Amish home built with dowels fitted horizontally across clothing rods. It stored fifteen to twenty quilts, rolled and wrapped with sheets. Use cedar chips in the closet to ward off moths and any other small creatures. Never store a quilt in a plastic bag, as it can sweat and mildew.

If you fold the quilt in half, and in half again, after a long period of storage fold lines will form. These fold lines will weaken the fabric, causing tears or holes. Refold the quilt at least every few months. If you have an extra bed, leave the quilt on the bed, covered with a sheet. Once in a while, unfold the quilt and leave it flat on a bed for a week or so.

Enjoy your quilts. Exhibit them, share them, display them on your beds and walls, use them, or give them away.

Appraising the Quilt

I have appraised quilts for resale and insurance purposes for over twenty years. Appraising quilts is more complicated than it may appear. The value is determined by a variety of factors: quality, age, size, etc. Quilts are appraised for insurance, to be entered into shows, and for sale.

I do not appraise quilts from photographs, as the photo may be poor, or the quilt may be poor and that doesn't show in the photo. The Actual Replacement Value is the amount set by an appraiser that he or she feels the quilt is worth. This is the amount that an insurance company would pay if the quilt was lost, stolen, or damaged.

Quiltmakers sometimes see quilts for sale and think that the asking price is the amount of money that they will get if they sell their quilts to a dealer. If a quilt is purchased for resale, it is usually marked up at least forty to fifty percent. Seek a qualified appraiser as you would for any art object. Ask at your local quilt shop, call a museum for a recommendation, or write to me.

The Patterns

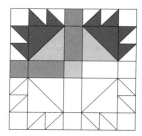

Pattern Value Definition

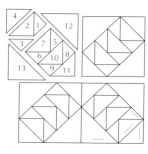

Piecing Sequence

Basic Grids used in this Book

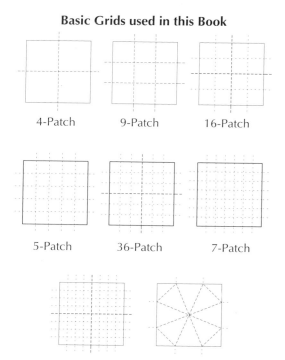

4-Patch   9-Patch   16-Patch

5-Patch   36-Patch   7-Patch

64-Patch   8-Pointed Star

How to Use the Patterns

Pattern Value Definition

Use the diagrams at the bottom of the pattern page and one of the methods listed below to decide on the fabric placement. Think about the value contrast, the color balance and the grain line when designing the blocks. Will the pattern be well defined with the fabrics you have chosen?

- Use a pencil to shade the diagram to indicate the values.
- Use colored pencils to indicate the color placement of the fabric.
- Glue small pieces of your fabric to the diagram.
- Determine how many pieces of each fabric to cut.

Seam Allowance

A ¼" seam allowance is used for patchwork. All blocks are sewn to 12½". All blocks are finished to 12". For appliqué blocks, the background fabric is cut to 13", and then trimmed to 12½" when finished.

Pattern Difficulty

The sewing level is indicated on each pattern with a thimble rating: 🎩 easy, 🎩 🎩 average, 🎩 🎩 🎩 intermediate, 🎩 🎩 🎩 🎩 complex.

Patchwork

- Trace the pattern parts onto template plastic or similar material
- Cut very accurate templates
- Mark the fabric very accurately
- Cut the fabric very accurately

Piecing Sequence

- Sew the smallest pieces together first
- Sew the smallest piece to the next larger piece
- Sew the pieced parts together into units
- Sew the units together into rows
- Sew the rows together
- Follow individual variations given on each page

Basic Grids

The patchwork patterns are divided into parts that fit into a grid. Each pattern states what grid the pattern is based upon. Patterns may be drafted to any size using a larger or smaller grid that is made of the same divisions as the grids indicated on each page. Or, use *The Big Book of Grids,* by C. Anthony & L. Lehman. This book is the best drafting tool provided for the quiltmaker. It provides full-size basic grids from 3" to 14" to use to draft any pattern. For information on how to order, refer to the Bibliography.

Reversed Pieces

Some patterns indicate to cut some pieces reversed; if you are using a print fabric, one-half of the total pieces need to be cut reversed or mirrored. This is done by turning the template over, thus reversing the pattern. Place the template on the wrong side of the fabric. Trace the design lines of the fabric onto the template with a permanent felt marker. Mark around the edge of the template. Cut out the fabric piece. Turn the template over. Align the marked lines on the template to similar lines on the fabric. Mark around the edge of the template. Cut out the fabric piece.

I make a mock-up or model of most of my quilts before they are sewn. This way of working helps me to see the value balance, color placement and overall pattern development. This is tedious work, and takes a long time. Beginners may want to work more spontaneously and not do this for their first quilt.

Photocopy the diagram on the next page, enlarging the diagram as needed. I use 3" blocks. Cut the copies apart and reassemble them, or make your own setting plan. Paste bits of the fabrics into the block to see what works well for you.

Photocopy two more complete plans. Use one for templates and keep the second one for a final reference copy. Arrange the blocks as desired. These are arranged in alphabetical order. Begin by pasting the fabric on one pattern or look at the overall plan. Use the model as a guide. Change the fabrics as needed during the sewing process.

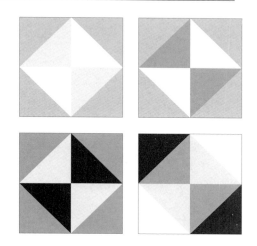

Paste-up for frontispiece quilt, by Diana Leone.

Paste-up for cover quilt, by Diana Leone.

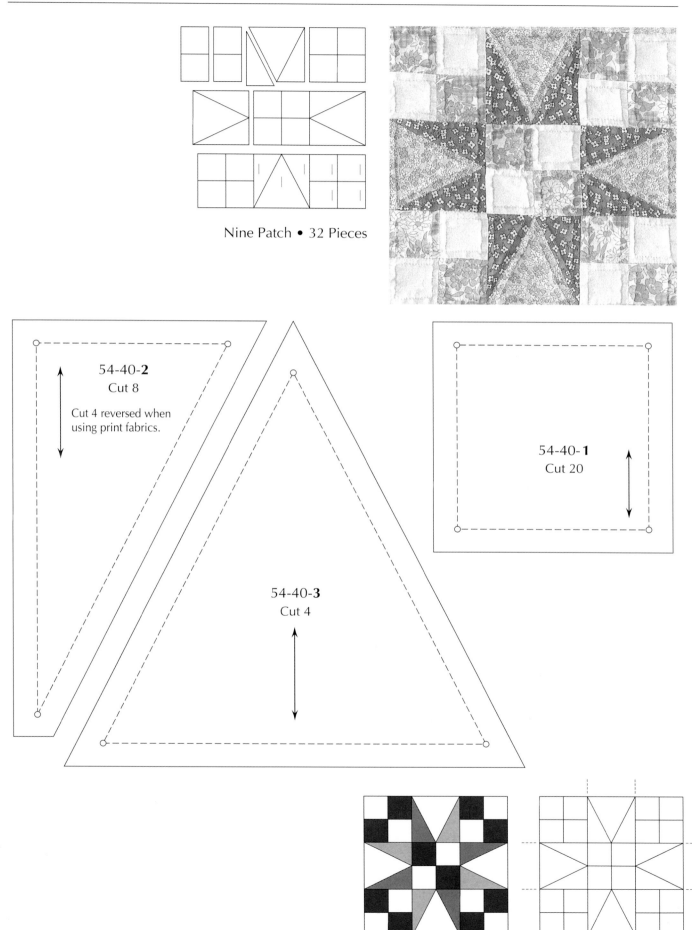

Nine Patch • 32 Pieces

54-40-**2**
Cut 8

Cut 4 reversed when
using print fabrics.

54-40-**1**
Cut 20

54-40-**3**
Cut 4

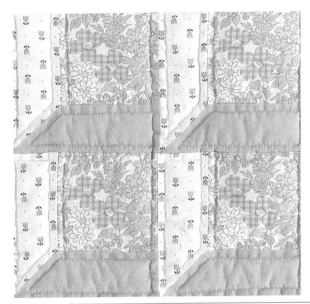

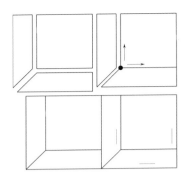

Four Patch • 3 Pieces

Use three different values to develop depth in the pattern. Light comes forward, dark recedes. Use one light, one medium and one dark in each of the three parts, and the pattern will have depth.

For complete illustrations and instructions see *"Attic Windows, A Contemporary View"* by Diana Leone.

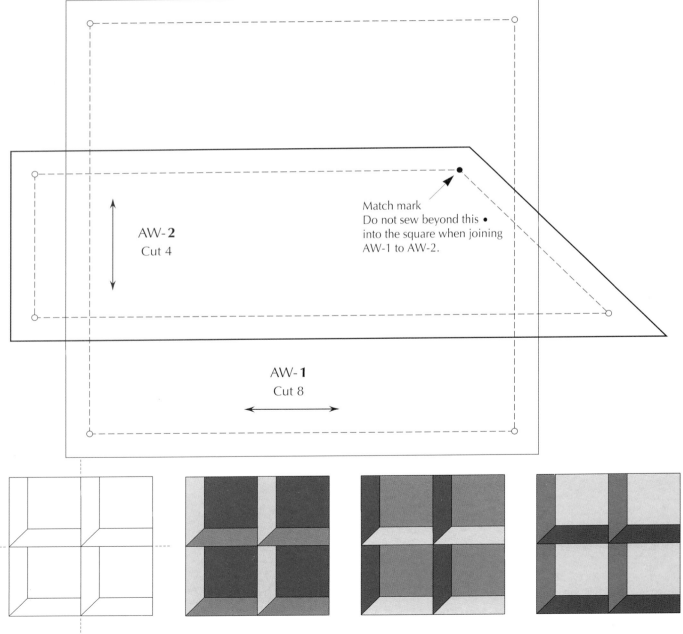

AW-**2**
Cut 4

Match mark
Do not sew beyond this •
into the square when joining
AW-1 to AW-2.

AW-**1**
Cut 8

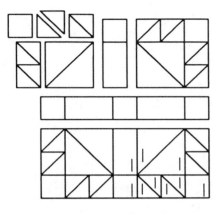

Seven Patch • 53 Pieces

Errata Sheet

Use the templates on this sheet for the 12" finished (12½" unfinished) Bear's Paw block.

The templates printed in the book will finish to a 10½" block.

We apologize for this computer-generated error, and regret any inconvenience this may cause you.

Page 12 Metric Conversions
Line 20, 30m should read 3.2m
Line 34, 12.9m should read 1.37m
Line 35, 90m should read 9.6m
Line 36, 9.6m should read 1m

Page 92 Attic Window
AW-1 Cut 4; AW-2 Cut 8

Page 118 Mexican Star
MX-1 Cut 8; MX-4 Cut 4

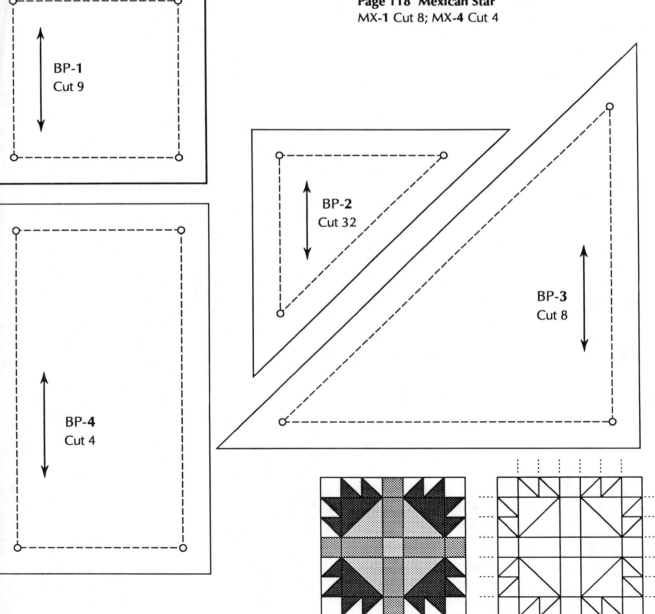

BP-1
Cut 9

BP-2
Cut 32

BP-3
Cut 8

BP-4
Cut 4

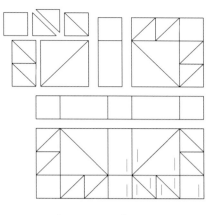

Seven Patch • 53 Pieces

BP-**1**
Cut 9

BP-**2**
Cut 16

BP-**3**
Cut 6

BP-**4**
Cut 4

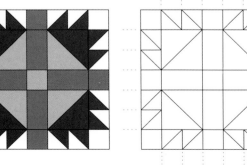

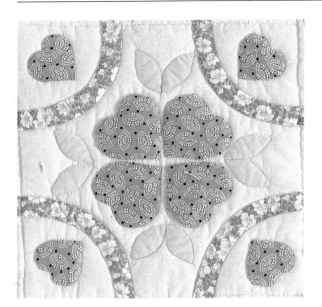

Appliqué • 17 or 20 Pieces

1. Cut one 13" background square.
2. Mark or trace placement lines on the right side of the background square.
3. Place a template on the right side of the appliqué fabric.
4. Mark around the edge of the template.
5. Cut the appliqué pieces adding a scant 3/16" seam allowance.
6. Baste the parts to the background fabric on the marked guidelines.
7. Appliqué using the basted edge or needleturn method.
8. Re-mark and trim the block to 12½".

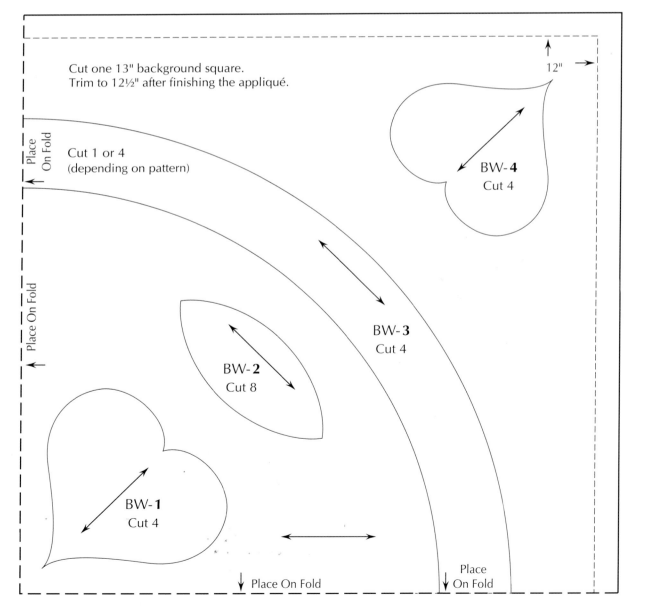

Cut one 13" background square.
Trim to 12½" after finishing the appliqué.

12"

Place On Fold

Cut 1 or 4
(depending on pattern)

Place On Fold

BW-**4**
Cut 4

BW-**3**
Cut 4

BW-**2**
Cut 8

BW-**1**
Cut 4

Place On Fold

Place On Fold

Place On Fold

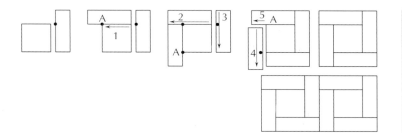

Four Patch • 20 Pieces

This method is called the "two needle method", because you can begin with one needle and leave it at point A. Sew the next strip on using a second needle. Finish the block with the first needle.

← Match marks →

BH-**2**
Cut 16

BH-**1**
Cut 4

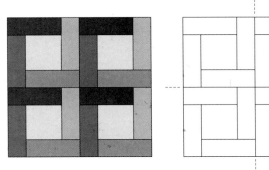

Nine Patch • 24 Pieces

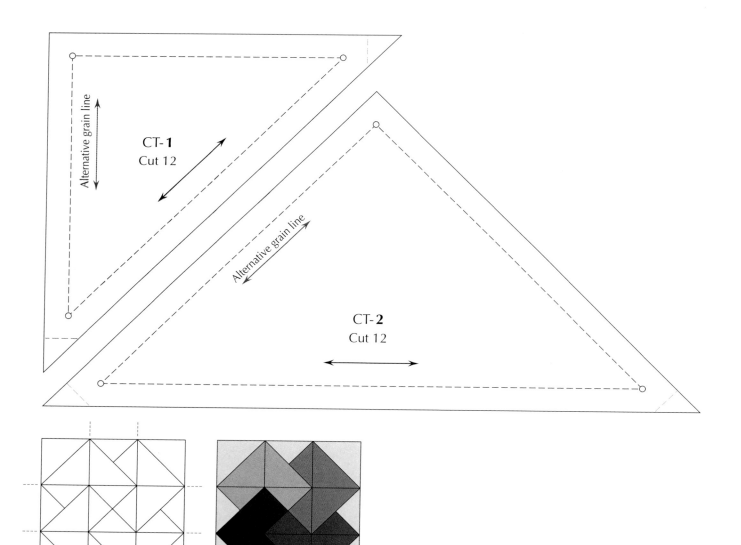

CT-**1**
Cut 12

Alternative grain line

Alternative grain line

CT-**2**
Cut 12

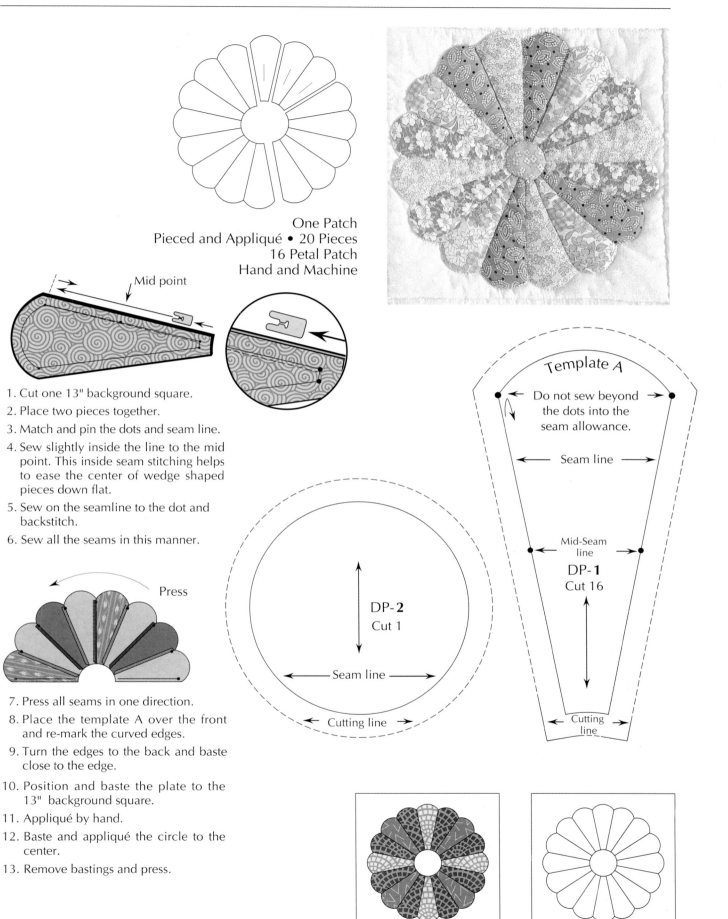

One Patch
Pieced and Appliqué • 20 Pieces
16 Petal Patch
Hand and Machine

Mid point

1. Cut one 13" background square.

2. Place two pieces together.

3. Match and pin the dots and seam line.

4. Sew slightly inside the line to the mid point. This inside seam stitching helps to ease the center of wedge shaped pieces down flat.

5. Sew on the seamline to the dot and backstitch.

6. Sew all the seams in this manner.

Press

7. Press all seams in one direction.

8. Place the template A over the front and re-mark the curved edges.

9. Turn the edges to the back and baste close to the edge.

10. Position and baste the plate to the 13" background square.

11. Appliqué by hand.

12. Baste and appliqué the circle to the center.

13. Remove bastings and press.

DP-2
Cut 1

Seam line

Cutting line

Template A

Do not sew beyond the dots into the seam allowance.

Seam line

Mid-Seam line

DP-1
Cut 16

Cutting line

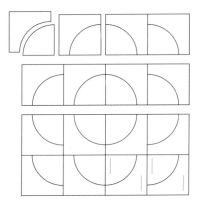

Four / Sixteen Patch • 32 Pieces

See page 48: curved seams.

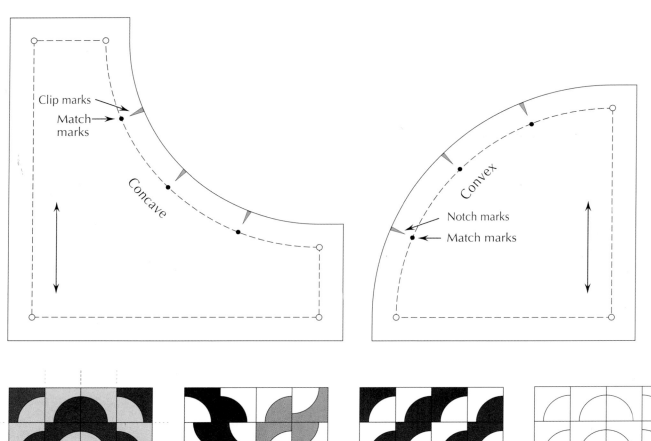

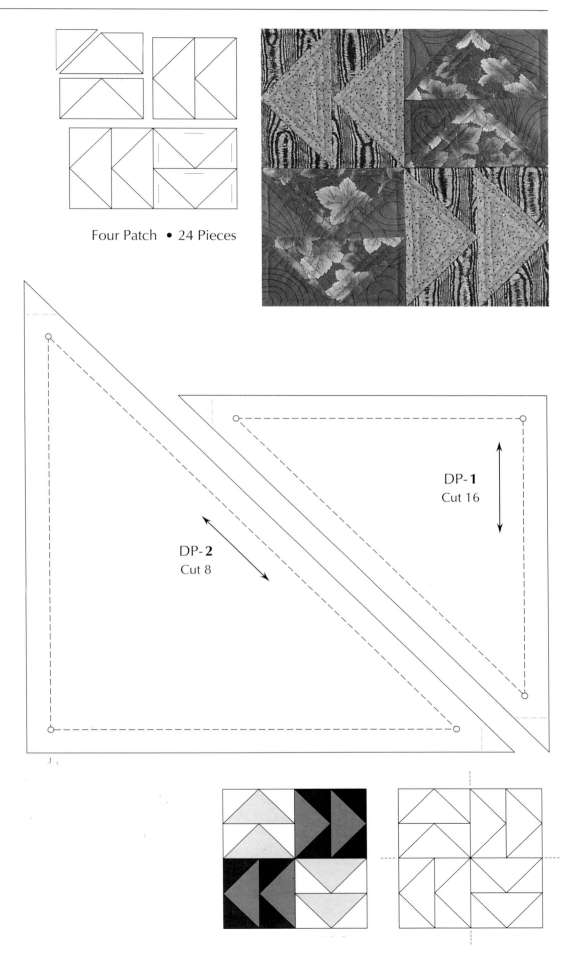

Four Patch • 24 Pieces

DP-**1**
Cut 16

DP-**2**
Cut 8

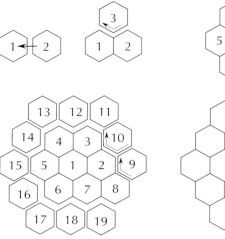

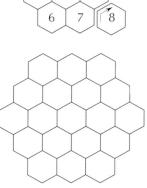

One Patch • 19 Pieces

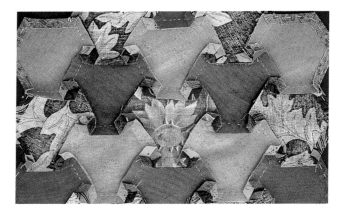

1. Cut one 13" background square.

2. Mark placement lines on the front of the background square, or fold the square in half horizontally and vertically and lighty finger press the fold lines.

3. Sew the hexagons together, beginning in the center. It is easier to sew this block by hand. Sew #2 to #1. Sew from dot to dot. Do not sew into the seam allowance. Sew #3 to #2. Sew the first ring or row around the center. Sew the second row around the center. Press.

4. Turn ¼" under around the edges and baste. Center the block on the guidelines and baste the block to the background square. Appliqué using the blind hem stitch (see page 58). Cut away the back of the block if desired. Press. Re-mark and trim the block to 12½".

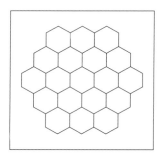

FG-**1**
Cut 19

Grain line depends on fabric and placement.

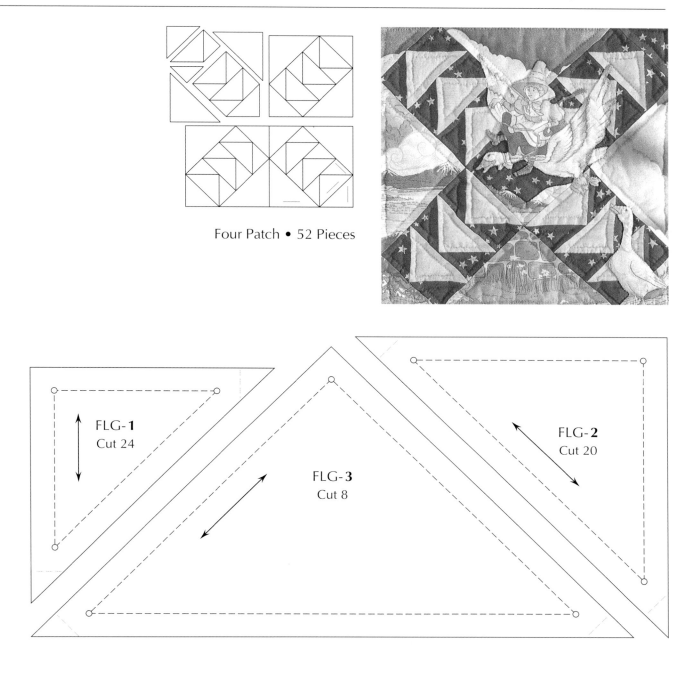

Four Patch • 52 Pieces

FLG-**1**
Cut 24

FLG-**2**
Cut 20

FLG-**3**
Cut 8

Pin as shown for matched seams.

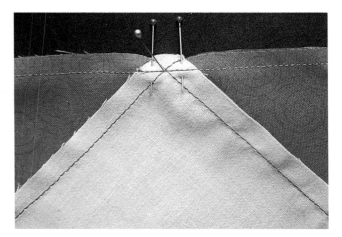

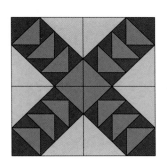

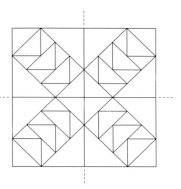

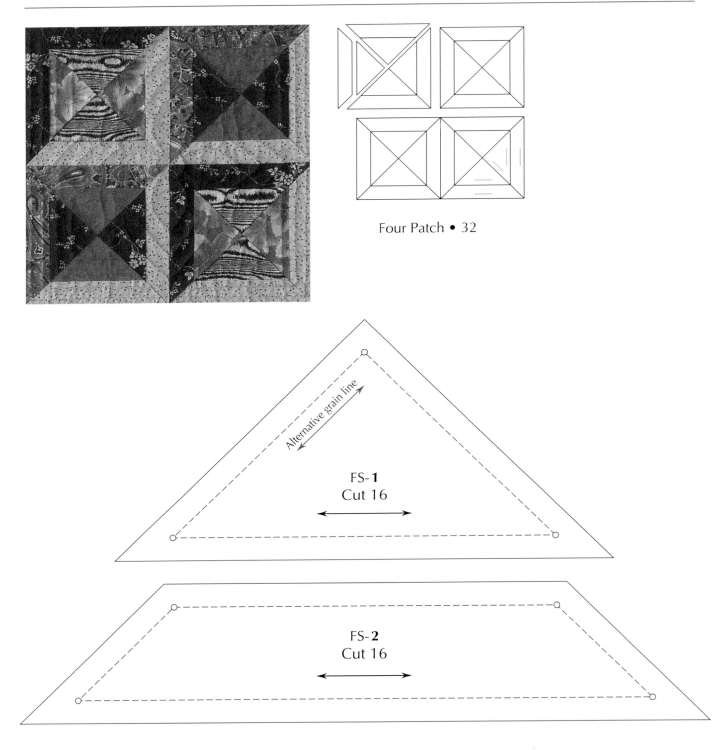

Four Patch • 32

FS-**1**
Cut 16

Alternative grain line

FS-**2**
Cut 16

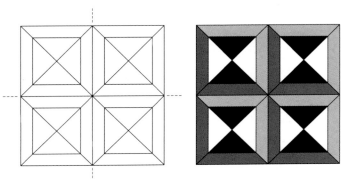

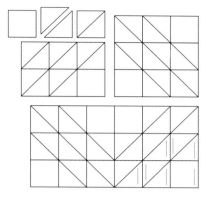

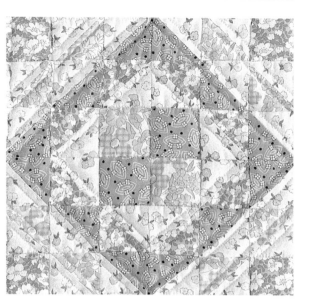

Four / Thirty-six Patch • 64 Pieces

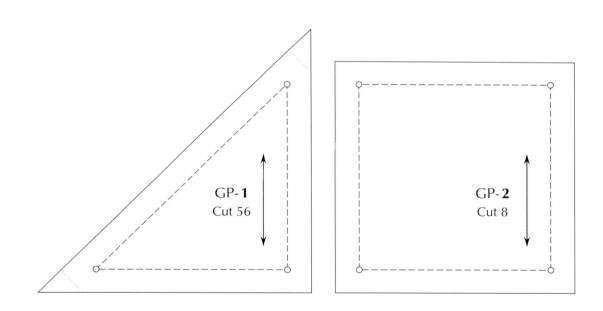

GP-**1**
Cut 56

GP-**2**
Cut 8

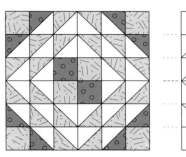

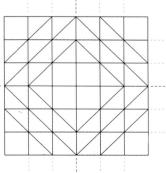

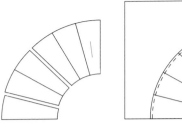

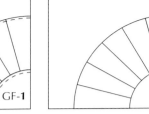

GF-1

Pieced and Appliqué • 8 Pieces

1. Cut one 13" background square.
2. Piece the fan unit. Sew from edge to edge.
3. Position and baste the Fan to the background square.
4. Appliqué using the blind hem stitch, page 58.
5. Position piece GF-1 over the fan and appliqué.
6. Cut away the background fabric behind the fan if desired.
7. Press, re-mark and trim the block's edge to 12½".

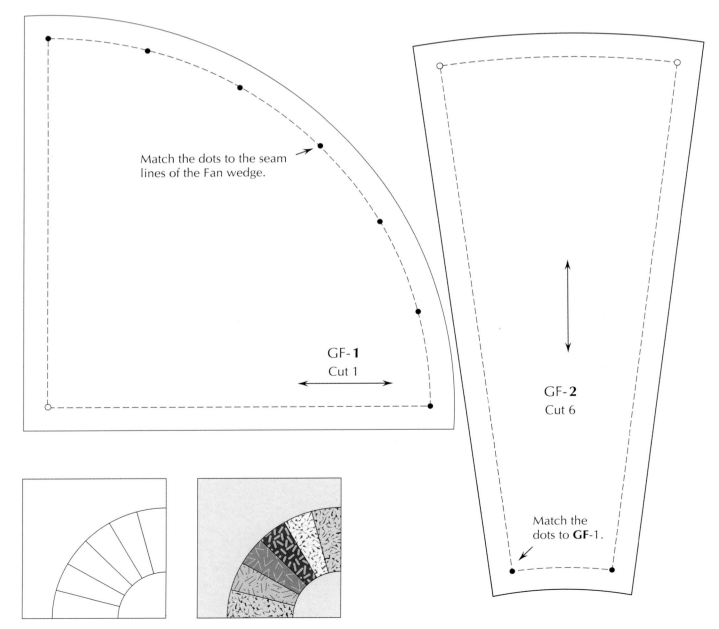

Match the dots to the seam lines of the Fan wedge.

GF-1
Cut 1

GF-2
Cut 6

Match the dots to GF-1.

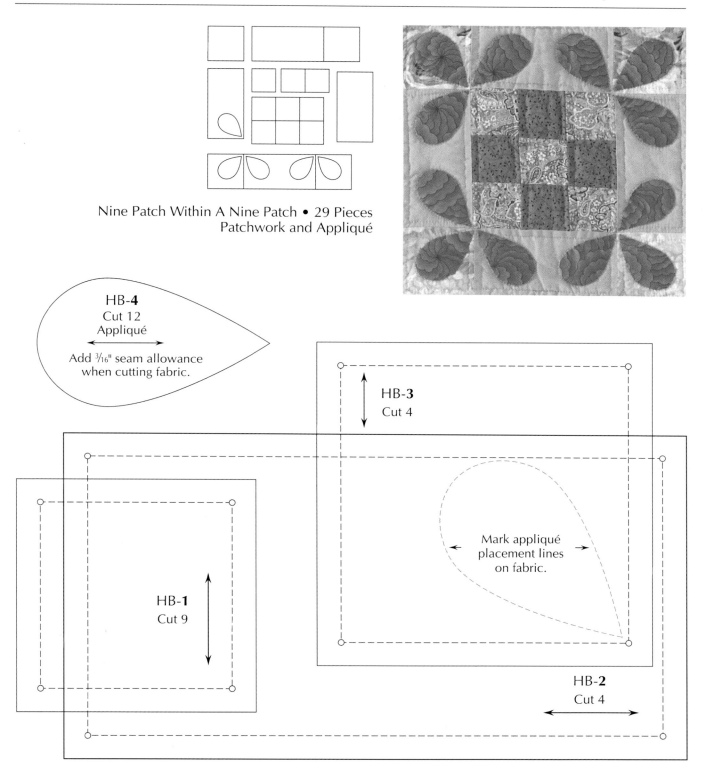

Nine Patch Within A Nine Patch • 29 Pieces
Patchwork and Appliqué

HB-**4**
Cut 12
Appliqué

Add ³⁄₁₆" seam allowance
when cutting fabric.

HB-**3**
Cut 4

Mark appliqué
placement lines
on fabric.

HB-**1**
Cut 9

HB-**2**
Cut 4

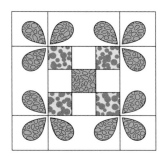

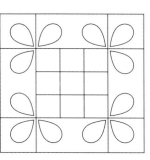

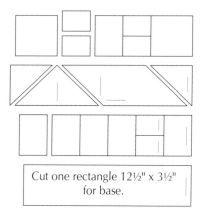

Cut one rectangle 12½" x 3½" for base.

One Patch • 19 Pieces

House quilt top pieced by Sondra Rudey.

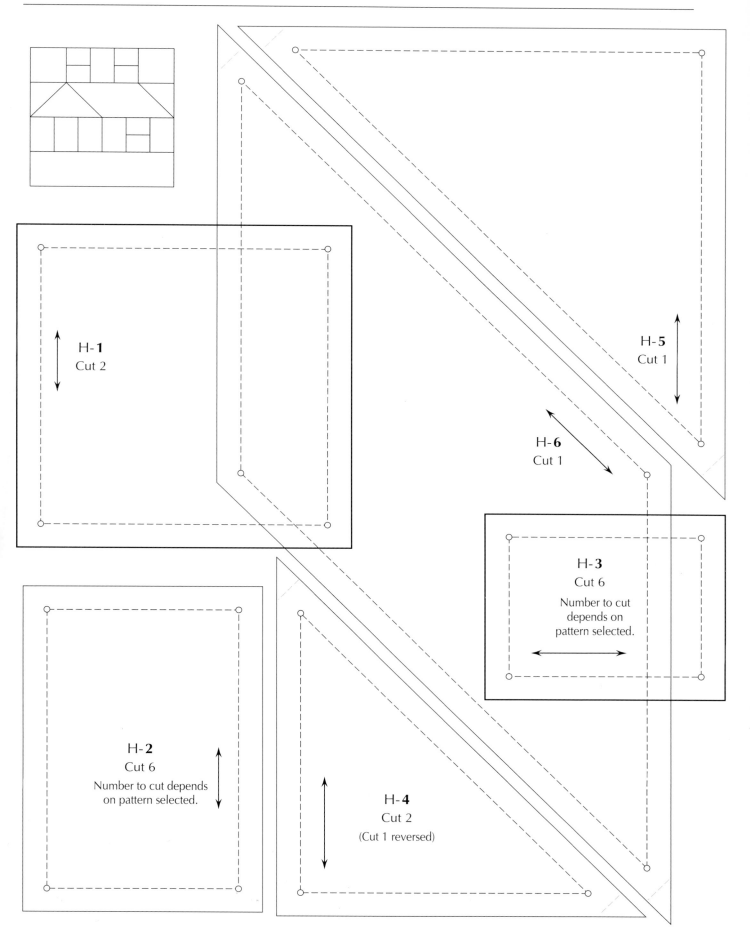

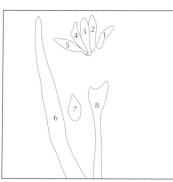

Appliqué • 14 Pieces

1. Cut a 13" background square.

2. Trace the appliqué placement guidelines onto the background square.

3. Cut out the templates.

4. Mark and cut the appliqué fabrics, adding a scant ⅜" seam allowance to the edges. Use the basted edge method, following the directions on page 57.

5. Position and baste the appliqué pieces to the background square, beginning with the parts closest to the background (#1-#8). Appliqué with closely matching thread, using the blind hem stitch (page 58).

6. Cut away the background fabric, if desired.

7. Press the block.

8. Re-mark and cut the block to 12½".

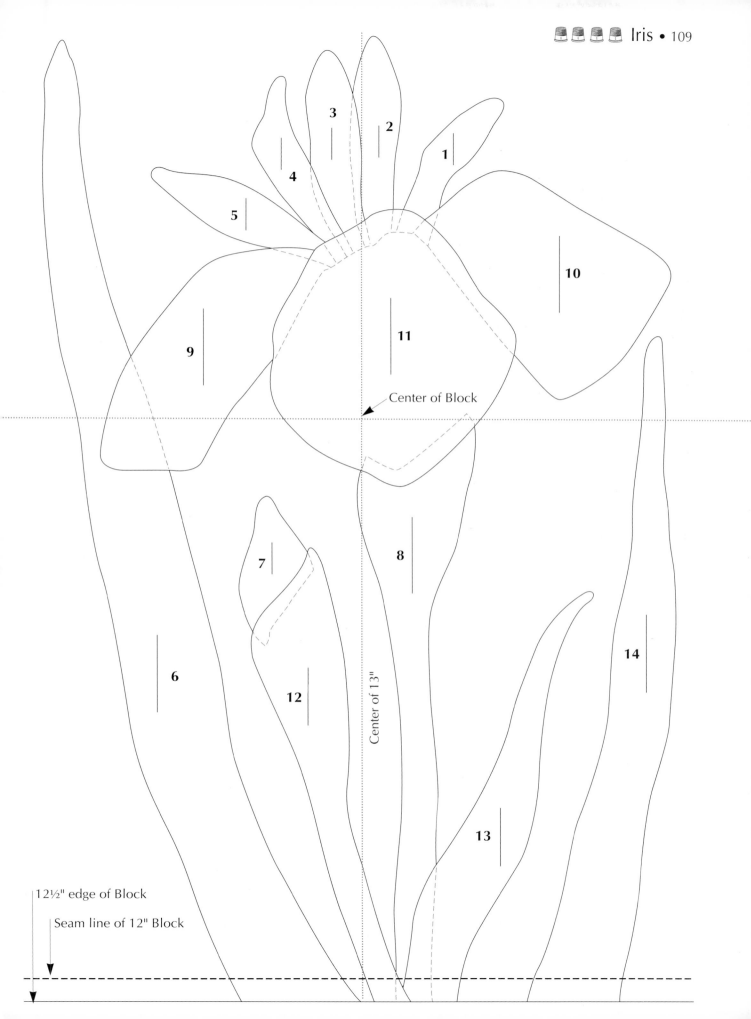

3

2

4

1

5

10

9

11

Center of Block

7

8

6

12

Center of 13"

14

13

12½" edge of Block

Seam line of 12" Block

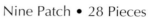
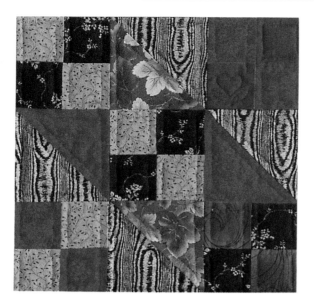

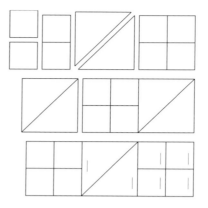

Nine Patch • 28 Pieces

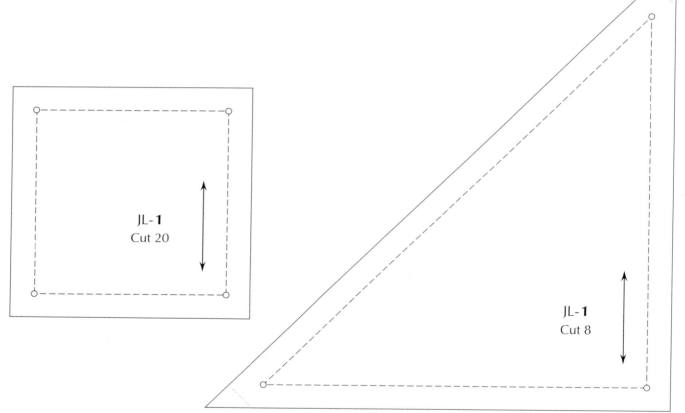

JL-**1**
Cut 20

JL-**1**
Cut 8

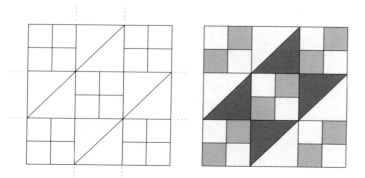

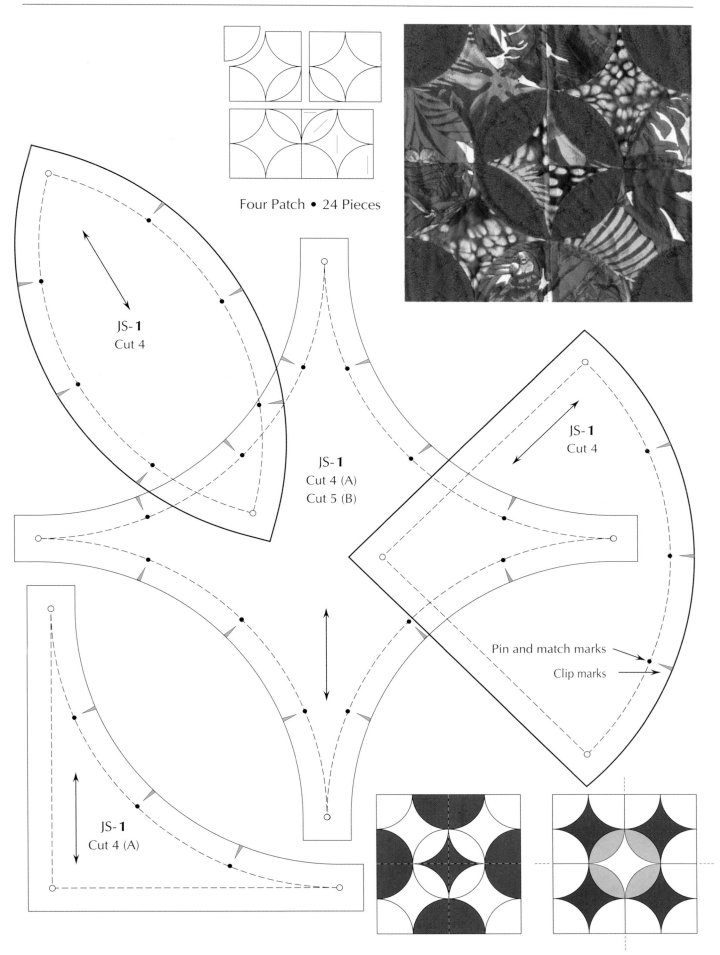

Four Patch • 24 Pieces

JS-**1**
Cut 4

JS-**1**
Cut 4 (A)
Cut 5 (B)

JS-**1**
Cut 4

Pin and match marks

Clip marks

JS-**1**
Cut 4 (A)

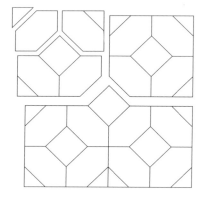

Four Patch • 31 Pieces

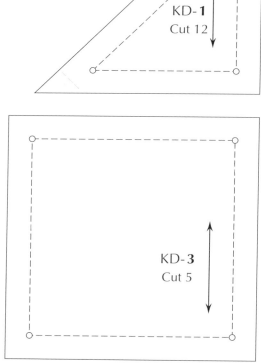

KD-**1**
Cut 12

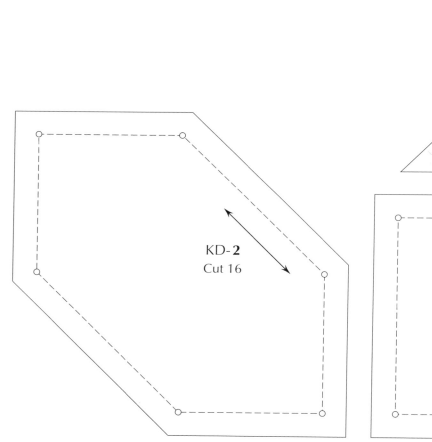

KD-**2**
Cut 16

KD-**3**
Cut 5

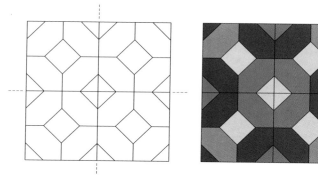

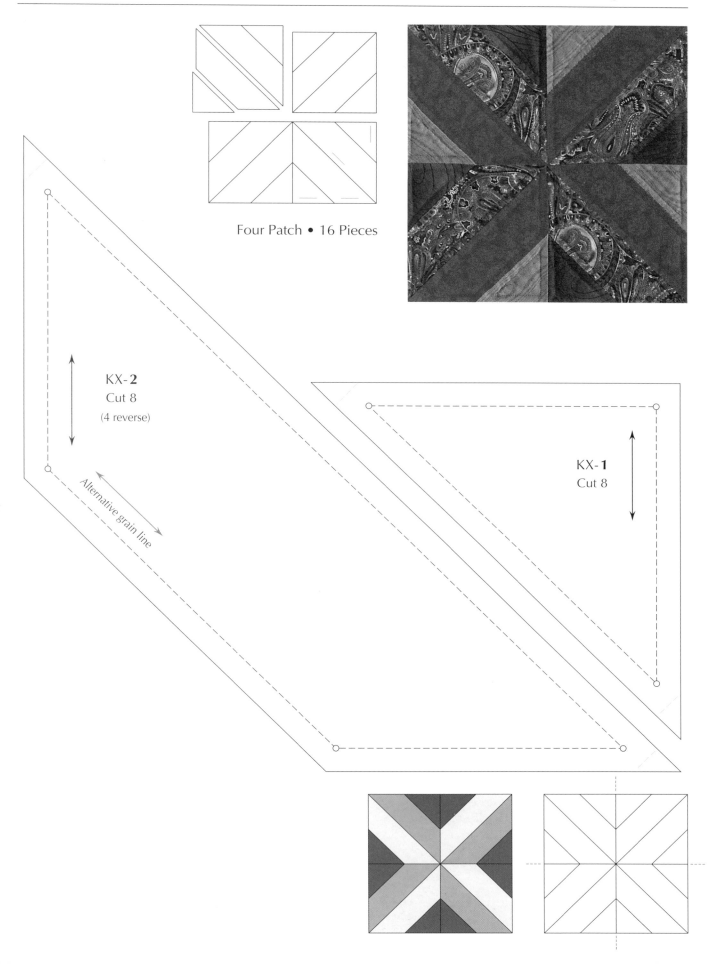

Four Patch • 16 Pieces

KX-**2**
Cut 8
(4 reverse)

Alternative grain line

KX-**1**
Cut 8

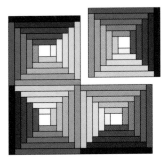

One Patch • 21 Pieces
Four Patch • 84 Pieces

Materials needed:
Fabrics: Lightweight muslin or batiste
Pencil
Ruler
Thread
Sewing machine
Iron
Rotary cutter, cutting guide and mat
Scissors

The Log Cabin pattern is easy and fast, and a favorite traditional quilt pattern. The pattern begins in the center. A square is cut and the strips or "logs" are sewn, right sides together, to the center square in a counter-clockwise rotation. The 12" block may or may not be sewn to a foundation fabric. The block may be made up of four 6" units or the block may be one continuous log cabin pattern sewn into a 12" block.

The Log Cabin pattern is a good scrap block. Use any variety of fabrics, divided into lights and darks. The center square may be cut any size, as long as when it is combined with the strips it makes a 12½" block. The strips may be cut and sewn any width as long as when they are combined with the center square the finished block is 12" square.

The center of the pattern is said to represent the chimney of the log cabin. Red is a traditional favorite, and used to represent the fire in the fireplace. Use blue to represent the sky, use gold to represent the sun, etc. The strips represent the wooden logs of the cabin.

The Log Cabin pattern is based on a half square. The block is usually divided on the diagonal into half light and half dark. There are as many variations of Log Cabin patterns as you can think of. Make one block for your Sampler Quilt, see how easy it is, and then make a bed size Log Cabin quilt.

A block pieced alternating light and dark is called "Steps to the Courthouse Square".

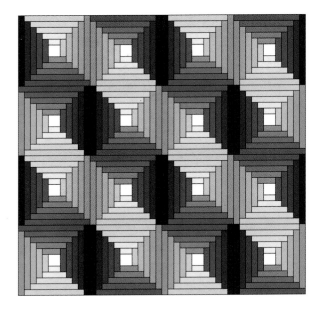

Interweave

Foundation Method

Cut four 7" squares of foundation fabric. An "x" is marked onto the square foundation fabric. The center square is aligned to the "x". Strips are cut from the light and dark fabrics. The strips are sewn, right sides together, to the foundation fabric. The strips are trimmed, opened and pressed. The process is continued until the square is filled with the logs. The "x" helps align and square up the strips.

The Log Cabin block may become a little smaller during the sewing process. You'll need a little extra because the thicknesses of the seam allowances will make the blocks smaller. To compensate for this, undersew the seam allowances by a few threads' width or a scant ¼" seam.

12" Square Made of Four 6" Squares

Cut four 7" squares of foundation fabric.
Cut four center squares 1½" x 1½" (1" finished center).
Cut 10 strips 1" x 42" of each light fabric. Cut 10 strips 1" x 42" of each dark fabric. You may need more of the outer fabrics—cut more when needed. You will need very little of the inner strip fabric. To create a light and dark side, separate the fabrics into lights and darks. You will need 5 lights and 5 darks.

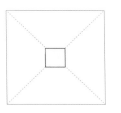

Use a pencil and mark an "x" from corner to corner on the foundation squares. Align the corners of the center square to the lines of the "x" and pin in place. Place the first strip over the center square, right sides together. Make sure that the top edge of the strip is slightly above the top edge of the center square. Sew from the top edge of the strip to the bottom of the center square ¼" from the edge. Cut the strip even, or just a bit longer than the center square (do not under cut.) Finger press open. Turn the block counter-clockwise ¼ turn.

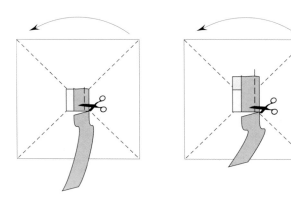

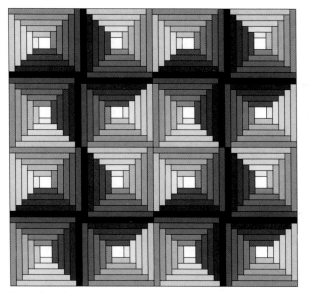

Pinwheel

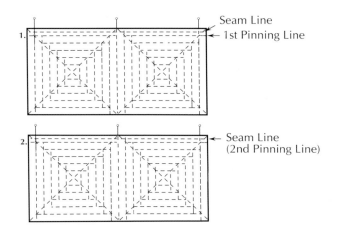

The marked guidelines will now become a very important tool to keep the block square and the strip width even and uniform. The upper corners of the first strip do not touch the pencil guidelines, but this first strip sets the pattern for the rest of the block. It is very important that the first strip is sewn accurately and straight. Place the second strip over the last strip sewn and the center square, right sides together. Sew the second strip, cut open and finger press. The left-hand corner should touch the line. Turn the block and sew the remaining strips, alternating dark and light fabrics.

Trim the foundation blocks to 6½" square. Place two blocks right sides together. Pin one pin straight through the corners of the second seam of the two blocks, aligning these two seams together. When aligned, these seam lines create the pattern on the front of the quilt. Re-pin the pins along the seam line, remembering that this seam can be adjusted to make the aligned seam lines on the block look straight. Stretch and sew as needed to fit the block together.

Repeat, sewing the units together, and then sew the two rows together, pinning and aligning the seams as you did when sewing the units.

12" Log Cabin

Use the template patterns. Cut as indicated on the template. Sew the block following the Foundation Method.
Photocopy the diagram below and arrange the blocks into your own design.
Piece four 6" blocks.

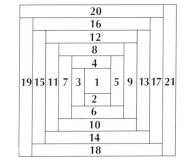

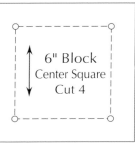

6" Block
Center Square
Cut 4

#1:1L	Cut 2	Cut 2	Cut 2	Cut 2	Cut 2	Cut 2	Cut 2	Cut 2	Cut 2	Cut 2
	#2:1 L #3:1 D	#4:1 L #5:1 D	#6:1 L #7:1 D	#8:1 L #9:1 D	#10:1 L #11:1 D	#12:1 L #13:1 D	#14:1 L #15:1 D	#16:1 L #17:1 D	#18:1 L #19:1 D	#20:1 L #21:1 D

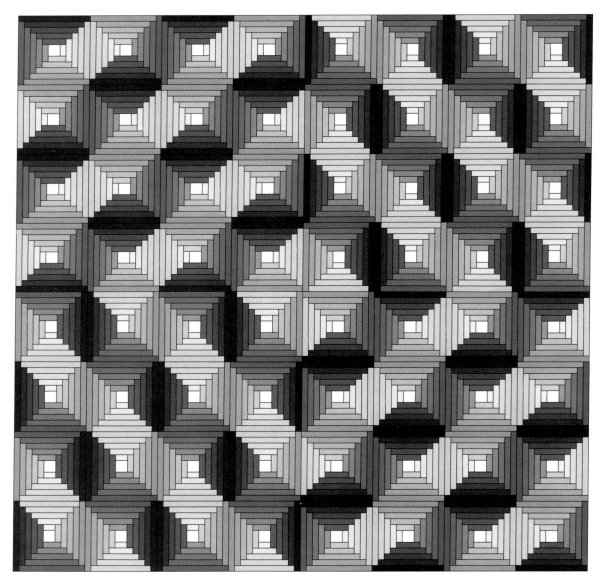

Trip Around the World

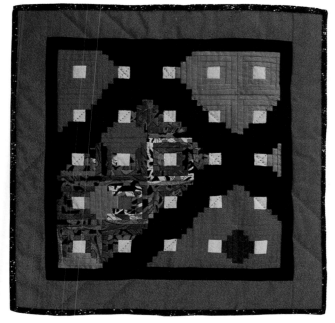

Contemporary Log Cabin by Kathleen Azevedo.

Contemporary Log Cabin by Kei Palmer.

"Monet's Waterlilies" quilt top pieced by Diana Leone, quilted by Doris Olds.

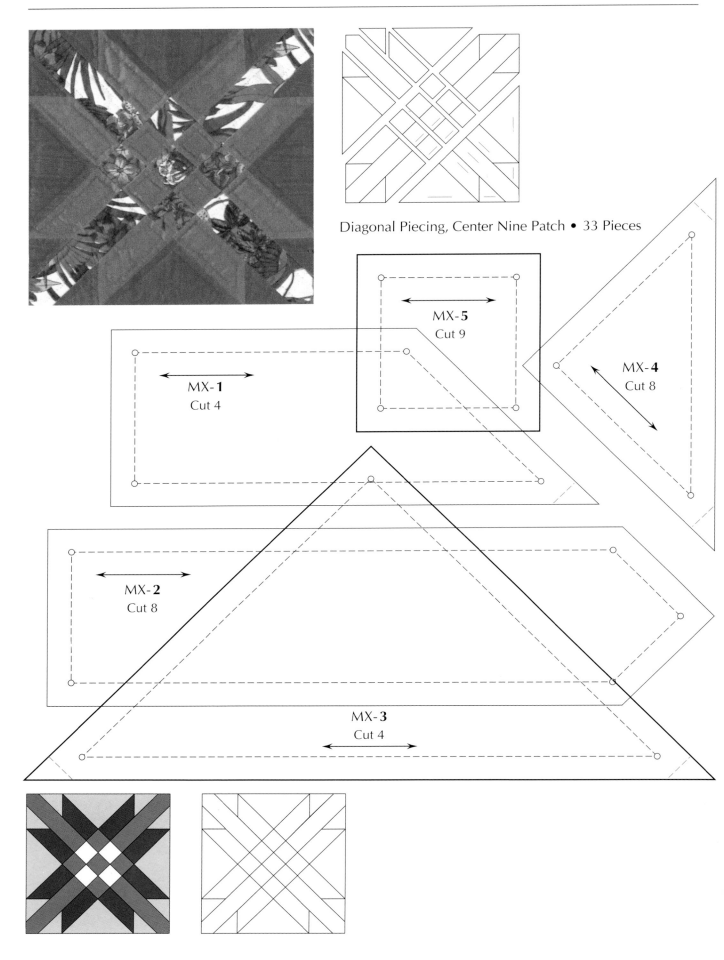

Diagonal Piecing, Center Nine Patch • 33 Pieces

MX-**5**
Cut 9

MX-**4**
Cut 8

MX-**1**
Cut 4

MX-**2**
Cut 8

MX-**3**
Cut 4

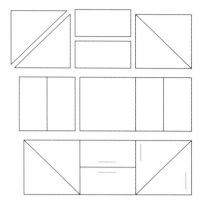

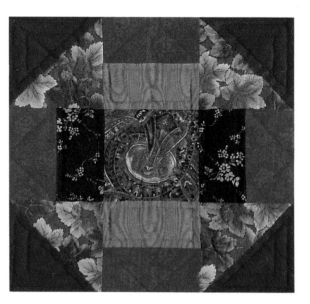

Nine Patch • 17 Pieces

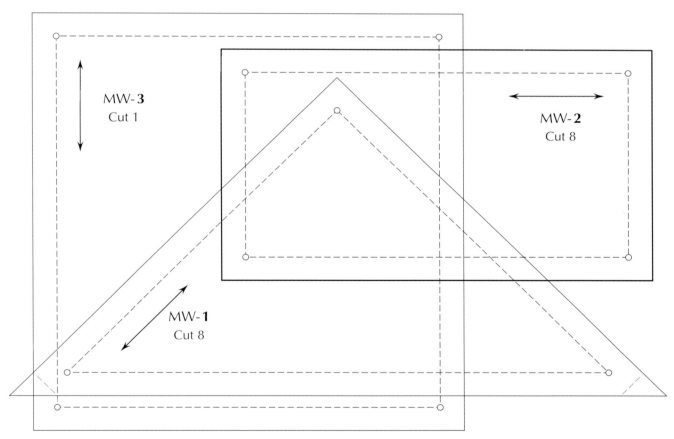

MW-**3**
Cut 1

MW-**2**
Cut 8

MW-**1**
Cut 8

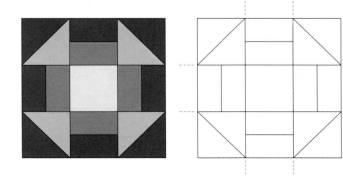

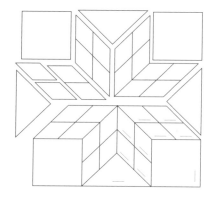

Four Patch • 40 Pieces

See page 47: sewing stars.

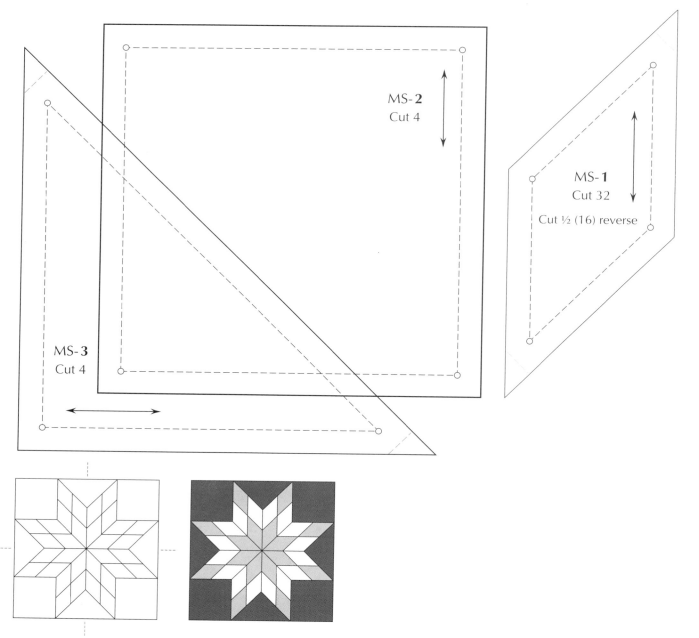

MS-**2**
Cut 4

MS-**1**
Cut 32

Cut ½ (16) reverse

MS-**3**
Cut 4

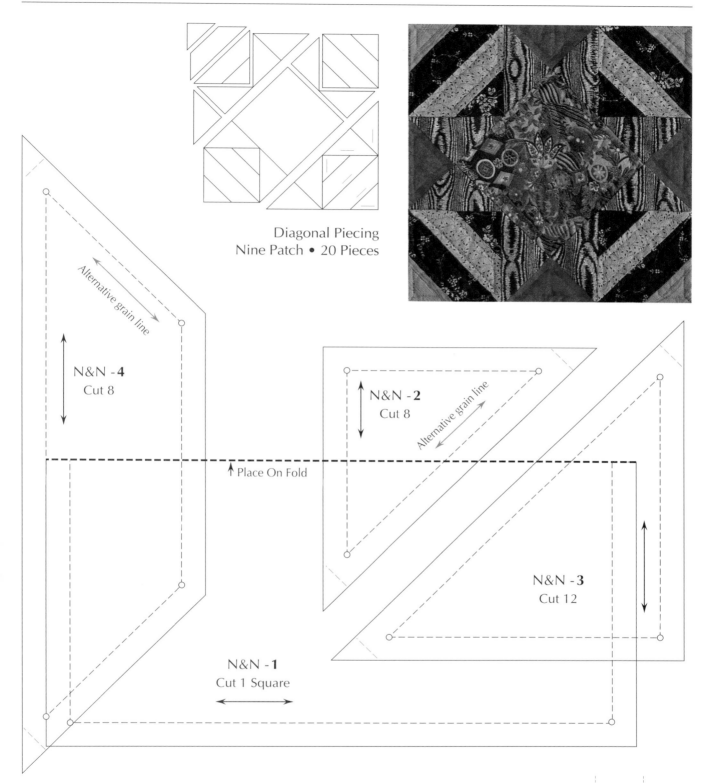

Diagonal Piecing
Nine Patch • 20 Pieces

N&N - **4**
Cut 8

Alternative grain line

N&N - **2**
Cut 8

Alternative grain line

↑ Place On Fold

N&N - **3**
Cut 12

N&N - **1**
Cut 1 Square

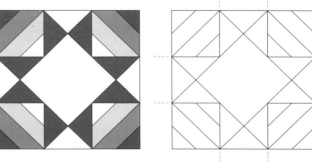

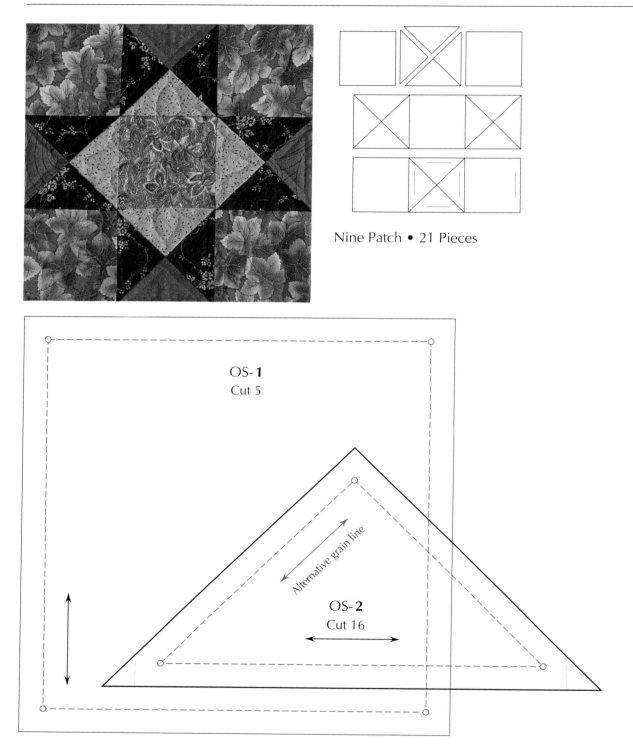

Nine Patch • 21 Pieces

OS-**1**
Cut 5

Alternative grain line

OS-**2**
Cut 16

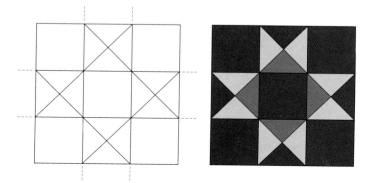

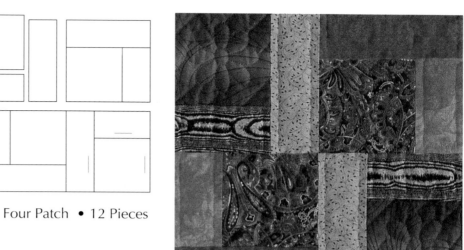

Four Patch • 12 Pieces

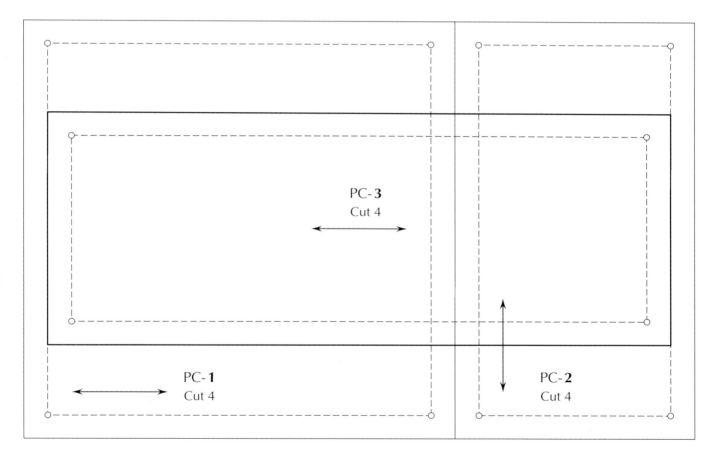

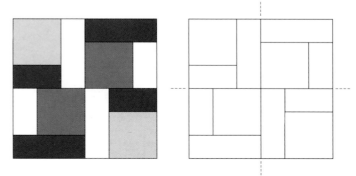

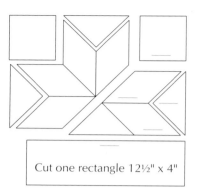

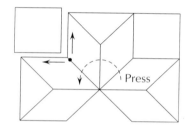

Cut one rectangle 12½" x 4"

Eight Pointed Star • 13 Pieces
One Patch with Appliqué

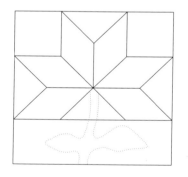

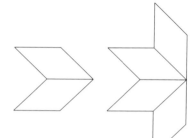

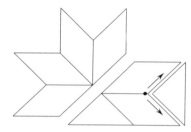

1. Piece the star parts. Sew the two smallest pieces together first. Sew the units together. See sewing points (page 47).

2. Set in the triangle. Sew from the inside seam to the outside edge.

3. Set in the square. Sew from the inside seam to the outside edge. Press the seams to one side in a circular manner.

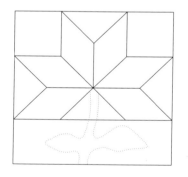

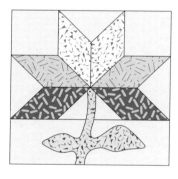

4. Cut one rectangle 12½" x 4". Sew the rectangle to the block. Mark appliqué placement guidelines.

5. Baste the stem to the background. Appliqué the stem to the block. Remove bastings. Press.

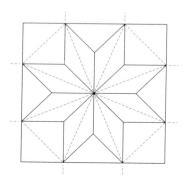

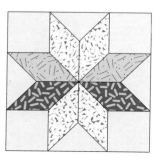

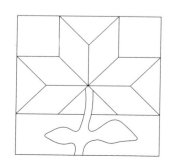

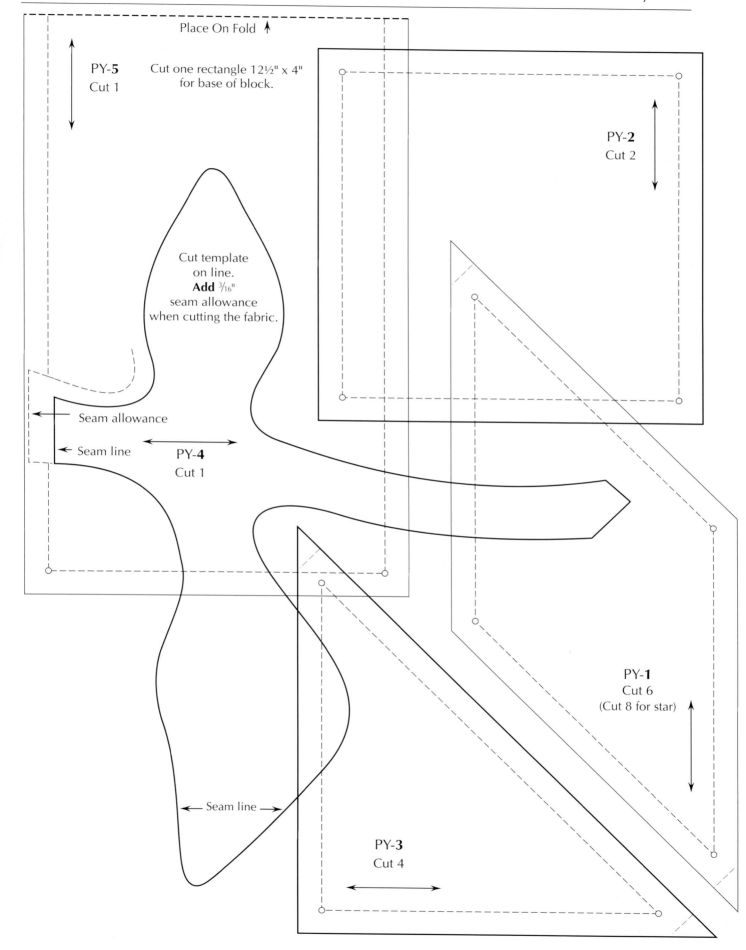

Place On Fold ↑

PY-**5**
Cut 1

Cut one rectangle 12½" x 4"
for base of block.

PY-**2**
Cut 2

Cut template
on line.
Add ³/₁₆"
seam allowance
when cutting the fabric.

Seam allowance

Seam line

PY-**4**
Cut 1

PY-**1**
Cut 6
(Cut 8 for star)

Seam line

PY-**3**
Cut 4

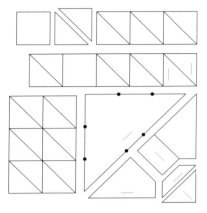

Five Patch • 41 Pieces

PT-**5**
Cut 1

PT-**2**
Cut 2

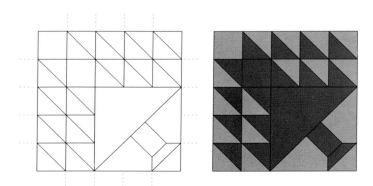

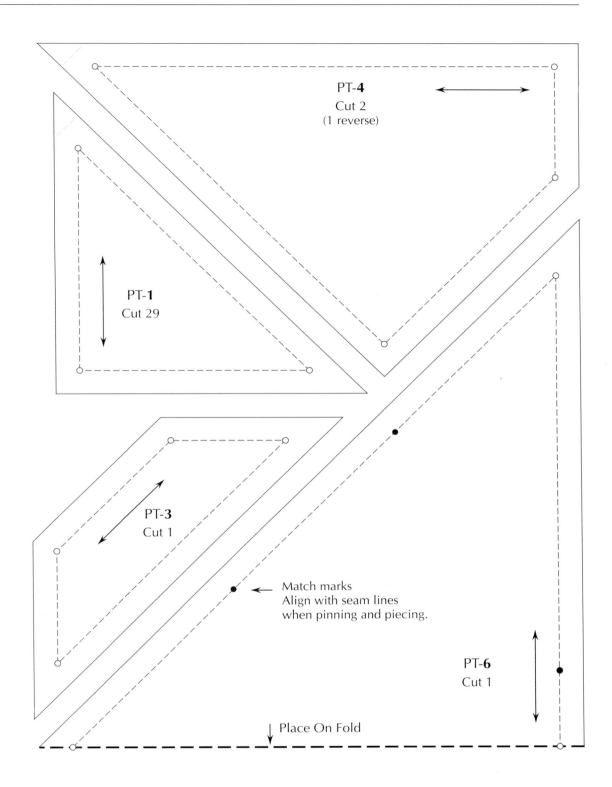

PT-**4**
Cut 2
(1 reverse)

PT-**1**
Cut 29

PT-**3**
Cut 1

Match marks
Align with seam lines
when pinning and piecing.

PT-**6**
Cut 1

Place On Fold

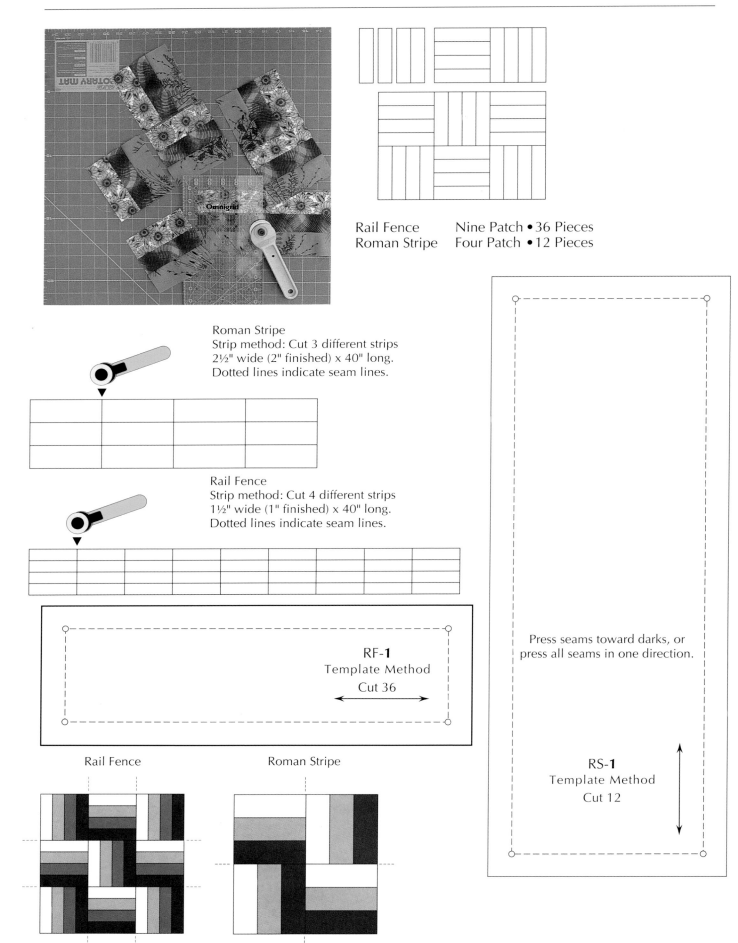

Rail Fence   Nine Patch • 36 Pieces
Roman Stripe   Four Patch • 12 Pieces

Roman Stripe
Strip method: Cut 3 different strips
2½" wide (2" finished) x 40" long.
Dotted lines indicate seam lines.

Rail Fence
Strip method: Cut 4 different strips
1½" wide (1" finished) x 40" long.
Dotted lines indicate seam lines.

RF-1
Template Method
Cut 36

Press seams toward darks, or
press all seams in one direction.

RS-1
Template Method
Cut 12

Rail Fence   Roman Stripe

Rail Fence pieced and machine quilted
by Diana Leone.

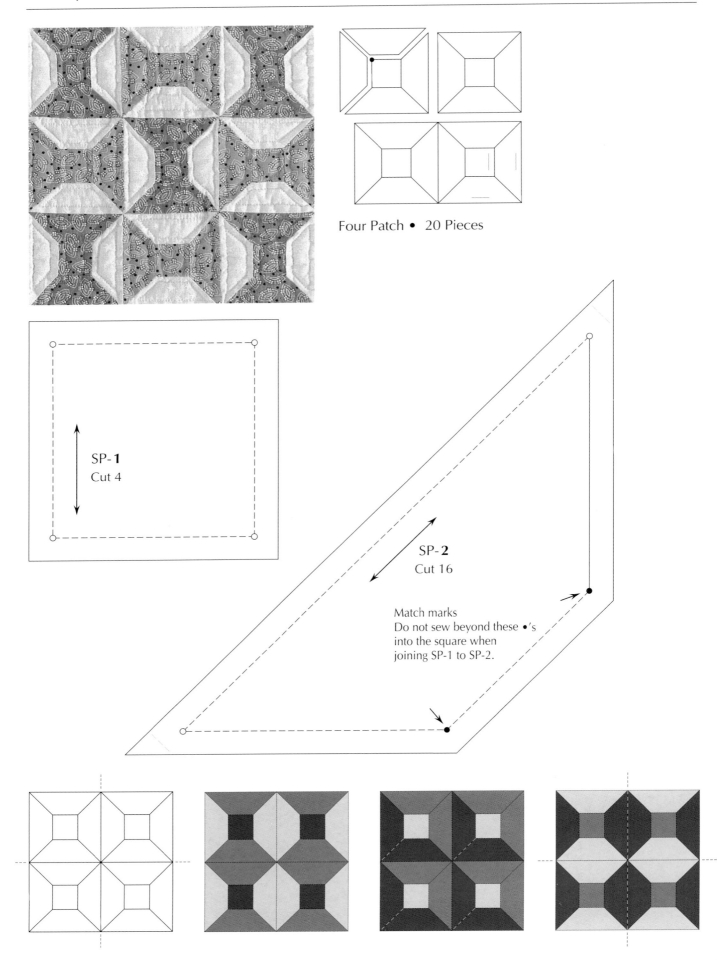

Four Patch • 20 Pieces

SP-**1**
Cut 4

SP-**2**
Cut 16

Match marks
Do not sew beyond these •'s
into the square when
joining SP-1 to SP-2.

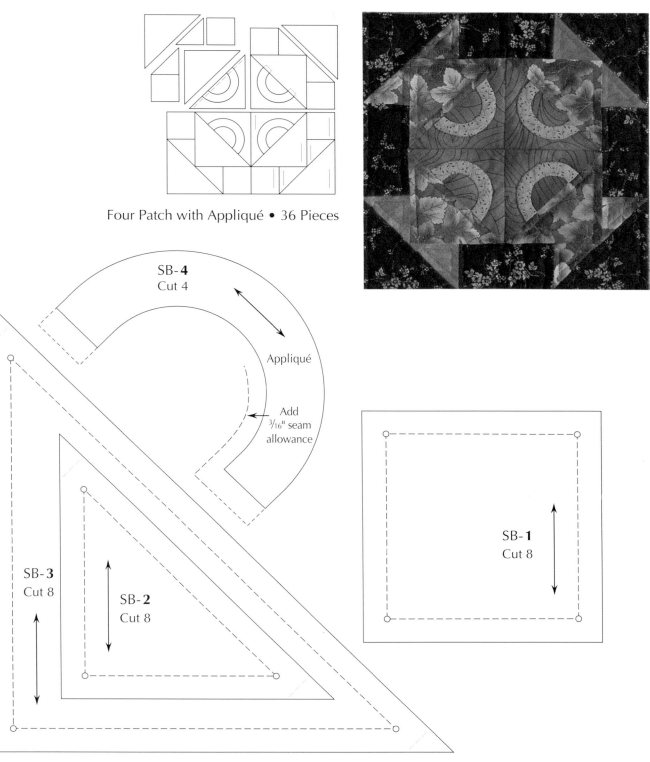

Four Patch with Appliqué • 36 Pieces

SB-**4**
Cut 4

Appliqué

Add
³/₁₆" seam
allowance

SB-**3**
Cut 8

SB-**2**
Cut 8

SB-**1**
Cut 8

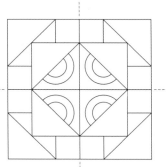

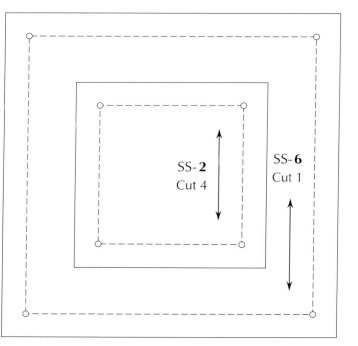

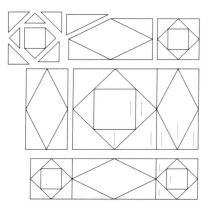

Four Patch / Sixty-four Patch • 65 Pieces

SS-**1**
Cut 16

SS-**3**
Cut 16

SS-**7**
Cut 4

SS-**2**
Cut 4

SS-**6**
Cut 1

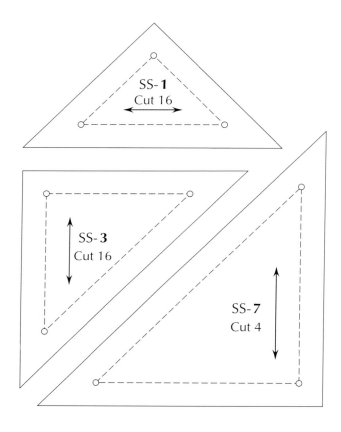

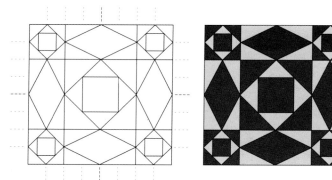

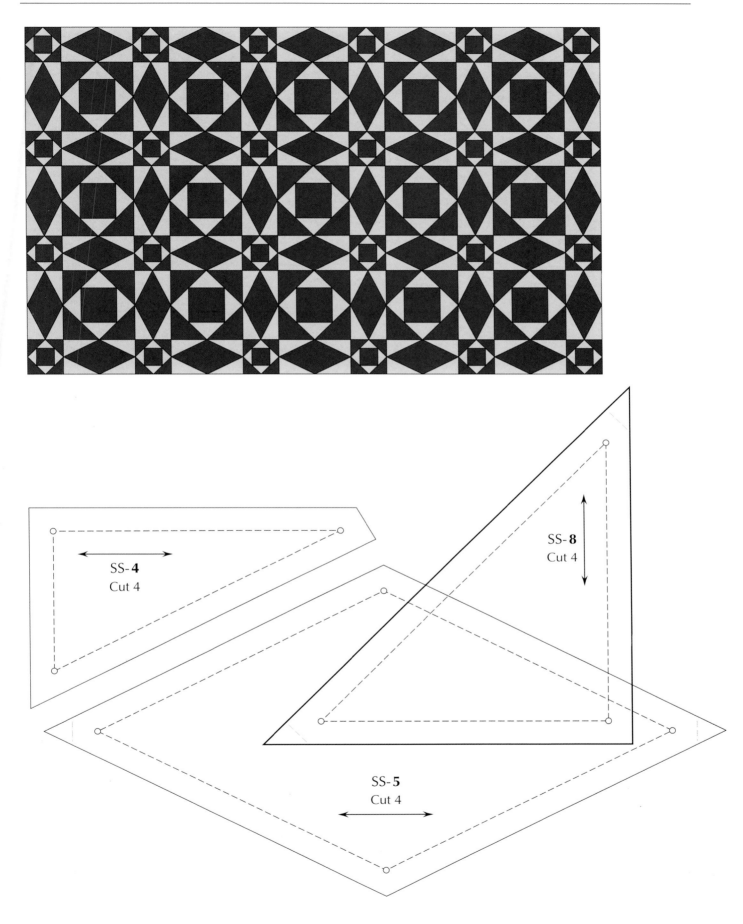

SS-**4**
Cut 4

SS-**8**
Cut 4

SS-**5**
Cut 4

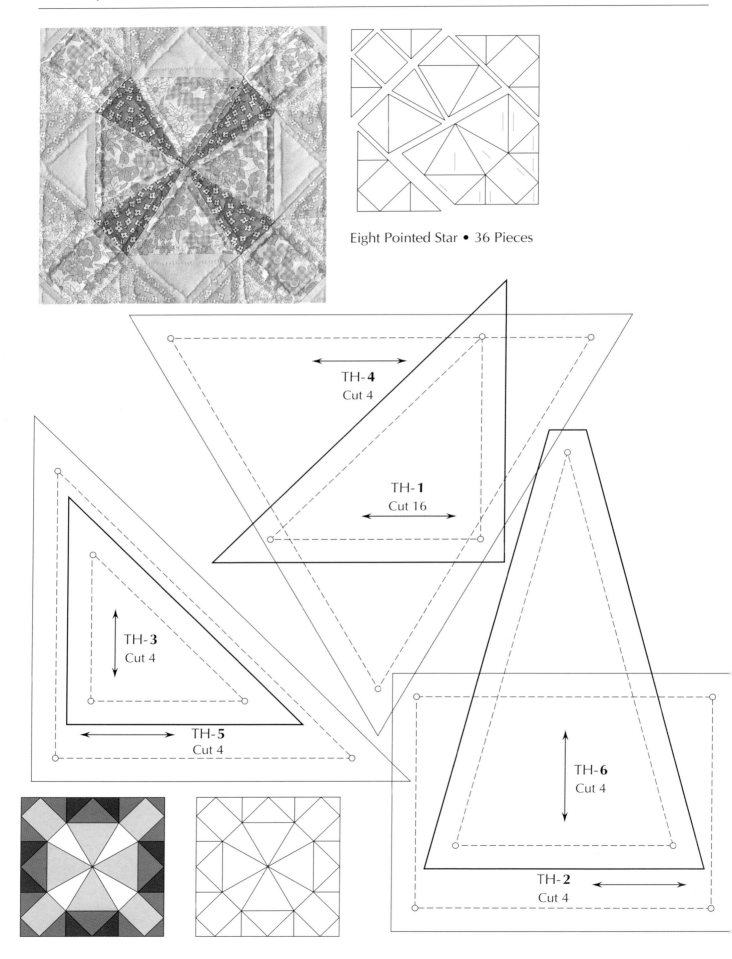

Eight Pointed Star • 36 Pieces

TH-**4**
Cut 4

TH-**1**
Cut 16

TH-**3**
Cut 4

TH-**5**
Cut 4

TH-**6**
Cut 4

TH-**2**
Cut 4

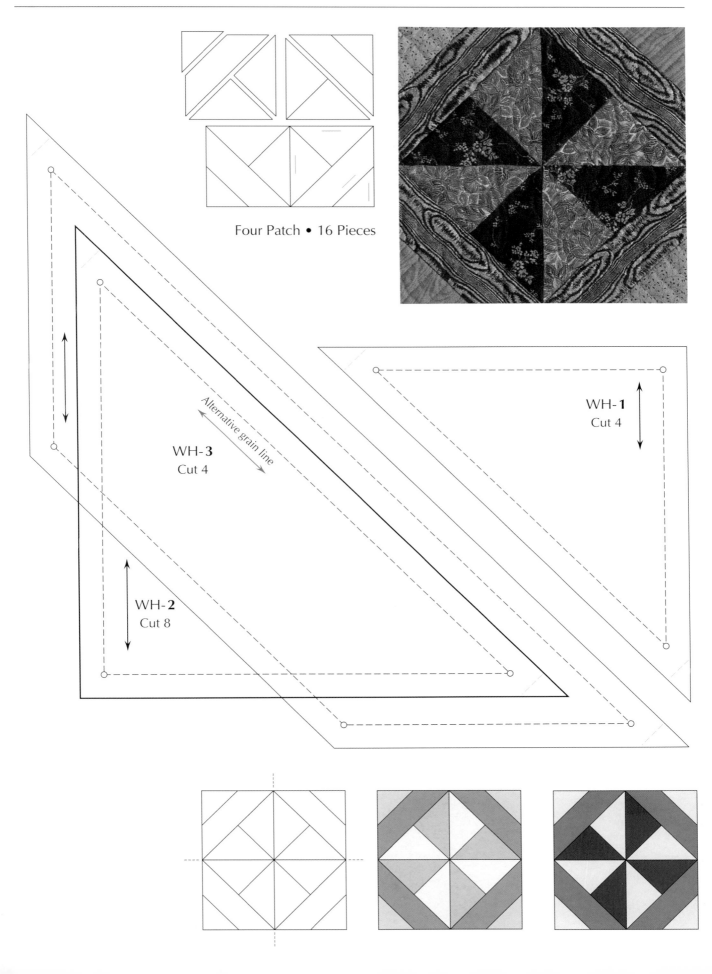

Four Patch • 16 Pieces

WH-**1**
Cut 4

Alternative grain line

WH-**3**
Cut 4

WH-**2**
Cut 8

Bibliography

Anthony, Catherine and Lehman, Libby. *The Big Book of Grids*. Mountain View, CA: Leone Publications, 1983.

Beyer, Jinny. *The Quilter's Album of Blocks and Borders*. McLean, VA: EPM Publications, 1980.

Birren, Faber. *Principles of Color*. New York: Van Nostrand Reinhold Co., 1969.

Bradkin, Cheryl Greider. *Basic Seminole Patchwork*. Mountain View, CA: Leone Publications, 1990.

Ickis, Marguerite. *The Standard Book of Quilt Making and Collecting*. New York: Dover Publications, 1959.

Itten, Johannes. *The Elements of Color*. New York: Van Nostrand Reinhold Co., 1970.

James, Michael. *The Quiltmaker's Handbook*. 1978. Mountain View, CA: Leone Publications, 1993.

_____ . *The Second Quiltmaker's Handbook*. 1981. Mountain View, CA: Leone Publications, 1993.

Leone, Diana. *The Sampler Quilt*. Mountain View, CA: Leone Publications, 1980.

_____ . *Investments*. Mountain View, CA: Leone Publications, 1982.

_____ . *Fine Hand Quilting*. Mountain View, CA: Leone Publications, 1986.

_____ . *Attic Windows*. Mountain View, CA: Leone Publications, 1988.

Martin, Judy. *Judy Martin's Ultimate Book of Quilt Block Patterns*. Denver: Crosley-Griffith. 1988.

Poster, Donna. *Speed-Cut Quilts*. Radnor, Pennsylvania: Chilton Book Company, 1989.

Rafalovich, Danita, and Pellman, Kathryn. *Backart: On the Flip Side*. Mountain View, CA: Leone Publications, 1991.

Thompson, Shirley. *The Finishing Touch*. Edmonds, Washington: Powell Publications, 1980.

_____ . *Old-Time Quilting Designs*. Edmonds, Washington: Powell Publications. 1988.

Books from Leone Publications

Attic Windows
Diana Leone
$16.95

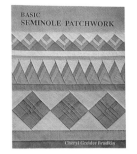

Backart
Rafalovich & Pellman
$19.95

Basic Seminole
Patchwork
Cheryl Bradkin
$19.95

Fine Hand Quilting
Diana Leone
$12.95

Investments
Diana Leone
$14.95

The Quiltmaker's
Handbook

The 2nd Quiltmaker's
Handbook
Michael James
$14.95 each

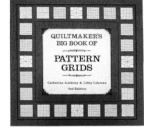

Quiltmaker's Big Book
of Grids
Anthony & Lehman
$14.95

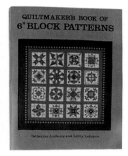

Quiltmaker's Book
of 6" Patterns
Anthony & Lehman
$12.95

Morning Star Quilts
Florence Pulford
Soft cover $24.95
Hard cover $34.95

Mini Appliqued Hearts
Sondra Rudey
$2.50

The Tied Quilt
Diana Leone
$2.50

For more information, send a stamped, self-addressed legal size envelope to:

Leone Publications, Dept. NSQ
357 Castro Street, Mountain View, CA 94041
(415) 965-9797   Fax: (415) 965-9799

Buyer's Source

All supplies mentioned in this book, and many more may be obtained by requesting by mail from:

The Quilting Bee, Dept. NSQ
357 Castro Street, Mountain View, CA 94041
(415) 969-1714

This store, owned by Diana Leone, carries every product available to the quilter. If there is something that you want, just write to us, and we will advise you as to price and availability. To receive a free newsletter, include a stamped, self-addressed legal size envelope.

Index

Pattern Index

Miniature Sampler Quilt made by Elizabeth Voris, 1980. The blocks measure 3". The work is hand pieced and hand quilted.

Miniature Sampler Quilt hand pieced and quilted by Elizabeth Voris, 1980. The blocks measure 3".